Musings from the Middle

John Y. Brown, III

Musings from the Middle

ISBN: 1483907341
ISBN-13: 978-1483907345

Editor: Bradford Queen
Cover art/design: Justin Burnette

I dedicate this book to my family, Rebecca, my wife, Johnny, my son, and Maggie, my daughter.

My musings are my own version, I suppose, of an Everyman's Journey through middle life.

We spend so much time trying to determine what makes our lives matter and what to give our time and energy to. At the end of our mid-life journey, we hope to have found our way home, or at least to have found a more enriching path for the years that follow.

For me, what I've learned is most important in this entire vast universe, is to have the love and respect of my wife and children.

Introduction

"Musings from the Middle" came about by happenstance. My good friend Jonathan Miller was launching a blog titled "The Recovering Politician" and needed regular contributors. I wrote a column for the inaugural week and then promised a follow up column every week. After missing my deadline several times, I confided in Jonathan that I felt like I had too much going on to meet a regular writing deadline on serious policy matters—and I added I wasn't in the frame of mind to write about political issues. I wanted a break.

Jonathan understood but, always the creative entrepreneur, a few days later had a new idea. He knew I enjoyed writing and suggested I just write for fun—write about whatever I wanted.

I thought I would outmaneuver him by suggesting I write about personal matters, family and observations I found humorous or interesting. But Jonathan said, he thought that was a great idea and the blog could use a light apolitical contributor.

I was stuck and said I'd do it. I am grateful I did. At first we did one post a week and then three and then five. Jonathan dubbed it "Musings from the Middle." The idea was I was making observations from the middle stage of life. Many posts feature my family: My wife, Rebecca; son Johnny; and daughter Maggie but also veer into general life and social observations. Some stories involve local political and civic figures. I include these because even though the reader may not know the individual involved, I believe they can still appreciate the qualities I try to highlight about them.

I have been privileged to live an interesting life. My grandfather was the son of a tenant farmer and grew up to serve a term in Congress and several terms in the Kentucky state house and senate. He was also viewed as Kentucky's premier trail lawyer during the prime of his legal career. My father bought Kentucky Fried Chicken in his early 30s and built it into an international franchise. He was a lifelong serial entrepreneur who briefly owned two professional basketball teams, the Kentucky Colonels of the ABA (with my mother, who was co-owner) and the Boston Celtics. He served as governor of Kentucky from 1979-83. I mention this to give readers background and context for some of the stories that follow.

Some entries are short, some lengthy and most in between. There is no particular thread to my choice of topics except everyday life and my attempt to find the interesting in the ordinary and the hopeful and humorous wherever possible.

I believe we all have a life story worth recording and sharing and that these collections of daily life stories make up who we are. Most importantly, these stories contain important life lessons and life-affirming –and often humorous –insights for others, if we take the time to understand and present them. And that, in a nutshell, is what I have tried to do.

I hope you have a fraction of the fun reading "Musings" as I had in writing it.

10

Foreword

by Donald Vish

Four fortnights before his 50th birthday, John Y Brown III, with tongue in cheek and pen in hand, wryly and dryly ruminates about how many more "youthful" indiscretions he might fit in before it's too late. Alas, it's too late. He can't think of any.

Brown's new book "Musings from the Middle" is a collection of insights and incites about the monumental and mundane events of every-day life.

Through scores of well-crafted essays, meditations, reflections and quips about family, technology, celebrities, food, travel, music, movies, and politics, Y 3 takes the reader on a life journey that includes details of his inept courtship plan upon meeting Rebecca, his future wife (he would give her his card and tell her to call him); the emotional ups and downs caused by his fluctuating KLOUT score; assaults upon his self-esteem based on a paucity of 'likes' on his business Facebook page; his ill-conceived strategy for backing up an iPhone with an iPhone (which he compares to "backing up a spare tire with a spare tire"); the liberating day of self-discovery when he removes "skiing" as his favorite sport from his Facebook profile when he suddenly realizes he has been skiing twice in the last 28 years; his personal victory over Demon Rum and his brash and brilliant revision to Friedrich Nietzsche's warning about the abyss ("if you stare long enough into the abyss it will wink at you and you will both giggle simultaneously".)

While the author appears in every anecdote, the book is not about him-- it is about us. Skillfully written with gentle humor and compassionate commiseration, the anecdotes catalogue the follies, foibles, delusions and illusions of the human condition as well as the victories and joys of being human.

John Y. Brown, III does not take himself too seriously. But his readers should. He is a thoughtful and thought-provoking essayist, a practical philosopher and wise man, armed with a disarming wit and, like Michel de Montaigne, graced with a humble personal motto: "I'm not sure."

Donald Vish is a Louisville lawyer and writer. He is president of Interfaith Paths to Peace and teaches Law and Literature at the University of Brandeis School of Law. He is a frequent contributing writer and reviewer for the Courier-Journal.

CONTENTS

What Do We Do Now?

When Jonathan Miller told me about his idea of starting a website called *The Recovering Politician*, I thought it was a clever concept—a partly tongue-in-cheek, partly insightful look at life after elective office. There is the famous last scene in the film *The Candidate* where Robert Redford's character, a charismatic underdog running for the US Senate, pulls out a narrow upset against an entrenched incumbent. Just before his acceptance speech, he ducks into a small room to avoid the throng of supporters cheering him on. He wants a moment alone with his campaign manager, whose sole purpose in life is to win political campaigns. The candidate, looking perplexed, looks up and solemnly asks, "What do we do now?"

It's an "aha" moment for the audience: what primarily drives some of our political candidates may not be the privilege of toiling over mundane public policy day in and day out, but rather to "win" some kind of overdramatized contest and the sense of accomplishment that comes with it. (Think of the hit TV series *The Apprentice* that follows job applicants for months going through a variety of ordeals until one is finally told by Donald Trump, "You're hired." We never find out—or care, for that matter—how the winner actually performs on the job.) Political candidates often get similar treatment from voters and the media. We treat business and politics as part sport and part theater.

But *The Recovering Politician* asks a slightly different, and more personally poignant, question: When one's political yearnings have been squelched, dashed, sated, or otherwise drummed out, doesn't every ex-politician go into that same small room—this time alone—and ask, "Now what do I do?" The answer, of course, is yes—and the choices ex-politicos make to create meaning in their lives post-politics is more interesting and hopeful than one might think. *The Recovering Politician* blog explores this area in hopes of humoring and humanizing the reader—and the subjects.

The metaphor of recovery for an ex-politician can be fitting. Recovery in addiction jargon connotes a bottoming out from debilitating excess that is followed by a rebirth that ultimately leads to a deeper, more wholesome, and more meaningful life. So there are parallels. Political aspirations aren't really an addiction, of course, but they can become an all-consuming obsession that can warp the priorities and perceptions of the individual harboring them and at times mirror aspects of real addiction.

Winning a political race is a powerful form of personal affirmation. Add to that the rush of crowds cheering you on, of striving publicly for lofty ideals, of battling societal wrongs, of pursuing the hero role, of putting it all on the line—these are heady pursuits that must rival on some chemical level a potent physical high. And it's a high that many may want to experience more than once—or twice, or—well, you get the idea.

And since most people who enter politics rarely fall within the middle range on any bell curve measuring normalcy in personality, isn't it fair to wonder if a small segment of society isn't predisposed to the potent allure of a politically laced buzz? Of jonesing for the next race, the next speech, the next press conference, the next burst of applause?

Personally, I think the answer is yes. And I reluctantly admit that I may be one of them. I've spent my life around politics and elected officials and have been an office holder myself for nearly a decade. My father won and lost races for governor and my grandfather ran for a variety of state and federal public offices—some 22 races according to family lore (losing more than he won).

So are you one of these people? I've devised a test to help you determine just that. These questions are drawn from a variety of recovery programs for actual addictions coupled with my personal experience and observations—and my overactive imagination. Answer them honestly.

You may be one of us. If so, you are not alone. And remember: recovery begins by admitting you have a problem.

1) Have you ever slept in a separate bedroom from your spouse because you had an overheated argument about healthcare policy?

2) Have you ever planned a family vacation in conjunction with the Republican or Democratic National Convention and pretended it was a coincidence?

3) Do you struggle to understand what "normal" is and seek to find out through polling data?

4) Have you ever had to apologize for insulting a loved one with a devastating line you heard a politician use against an opponent?

5) Have friends or family ever discouraged you from running for political office? (Two points if your friends and family were seated in a circle around you and took turns reading the reasons why you shouldn't run from a pre-written statement while a therapist moderated.)

6) Do others sometimes drink to excess in your presence to make you and your political conversation more bearable?

7)   While holding public office, did you ever call your family together and ask if they'd like you to leave politics to spend more time with them and were told they were fine with you away from home and wanted to keep it that way?

8)   Did you secretly cheer for Reese Witherspoon's ruthless character, Tracy Flick, in the movie *Election* when she ran for student body president because you felt "Tracy deserves to win" and will know how to "get things done"?

9)   Have you ever planned a political comeback strategy while still in the middle of current campaign?

10) Has a friend ever told you that she was going to support your opponent because "I can vote for you next time you run for office"?

11) When asked to list an inspirational movie in your political profile, did you put down *Braveheart* because you thought it would impress voters even though you slept through most of it and still don't know why Mel Gibson was painted blue during the scene that woke you?

12) Has your campaign manager ever greeted you with the words, "Looks like somebody could use a hug"? (Two points if you responded, "Yes, I sure could" and obliged. Three points if this has happened to you more than once.)

RESULTS:

If you received one to five points, you may have an underlying political pathology that requires bottoming out before you can begin the road to recovery. You are considered "at risk."

If you received six or more points, you are definitely in the right place. You have probably already bottomed out. But there is hope for you. Just not a lot.. But keep reading anyway. We're searching for success stories of recovery from politics.

And let's face it, each day you are reading hopeful blog posts is one more day that you aren't planning your next run for political office.

That's a start—for you and your loved ones. One day at a time.

Oh, and if you scored 15 points and haven't run for political office in over a year, please contact me. I'm looking for a sponsor.

My Road Rage Solution

Early this morning I realized I was in the wrong lane and was about to miss my turn. I quickly turned on my blinker and slid over to the next lane in time to turn.

However, the driver behind me was not only frustrated by my last-minute lane switch, but also felt the need to express her displeasure audibly by laying on her car horn several times. One short perfunctory honk followed by a series of three very long dramatic honks that created a melody of disgust toward me as well as seeming to foreshadow some sort of revenge being plotted against me.

I waved in my rear-view mirror that I was very sorry and appreciated her generous and courteous allowance for me to cut in front of her while at the same time duly noting her understandable frustration.

I hoped that would be the end of our exchange but had that anxious feeling that characters in horror movies get when they sense they are being followed by someone or something wanting to do them bodily harm.

After about a mile I recognized the car that had pulled up beside me and was hovering –and the driver, an attractive but visibly agitated blond-haired woman, waving her hands as if to say, "I hate everything about you for cutting in front of me a mile back and need to make sure you understand this on a deep and personal level."

I looked apologetically at her again mouthed, "I am very sorry" and lurched forward. She lurched forward too and became more demonstrative with her displeasure.

Obviously, I had been wrong for cutting in front of her, but the overreaction was becoming concerning.

I acknowledged her again but then tried to trick her into backing off by pretending I recognized her and gave her a friendly and enthusiastic wave. That is not the reaction she was looking for and she stayed next to me motioning her frustration that I wasn't "getting it."

Then I had a novel idea. I held up my left hand and pointed to my ring finger and mouthed the words. "I am married. I am flattered that you are interested but I am not available. Sorry." I then shook my head in mock disgust and drove off.

She was so stunned by my seeming confusion that she slowed to what seemed like a stop as I watched her baffled look fade in my rearview mirror.

Dumpster Diving

Yesterday morning, I stopped for coffee. It was still dark out. I was wearing a suit and, as usual, had thrown my tie in the passenger seat to put on later. I parked near a dumpster and before leaving decided to toss out some old papers piled in my front seat.

When I get to my first business meeting, I couldn't find my tie. Obviously, I'd accidentally thrown it in the dumpster and was very bummed.

Later that day I told my business partner what happened. She chuckled and helpfully suggested I go back tomorrow to see if it was still there.

So, I did.

This morning at 6:45am, I pull into the same place. The only other people outside in the parking lot were two women in tennis outfits talking to one another.

I get out of my car and walk over to the dumpster and lift up the top, which drops to the side making a loud clanging noise.

The two women stop talking and want to see what's going on.

I look inside the dumpster and see my tie. I bend over and reach in for it. After several swipes, I finally fish it out. I hold the tie up to look at it, sniff it and then brush it off.

The two women are now watching me in silent disbelief.

The tie was still in good condition, so I walk back to my car, open the door and drop it in the front seat.

As I walk back by the two women, they remain speechless and I'm too embarrassed to even make eye contact. I start to tell them what happened but decide it's too complicated and best to just let them draw their own conclusions.

1 Once Was a Millionaire

I recently found out that a little over 40 years ago – for about a year – I was a bona fide millionaire. I had no idea and now find myself reflecting on that year—"My Big Year" and asking myself, what went wrong and what can I learn from it?

In 1971 my father sold his controlling interest in Kentucky Fried Chicken. He made a good deal of money and, as I recently learned, created a $1 million trust for each of his three children (my two sisters Sissy and Sandy and me).

It was a surprise hearing about this all these years later since my father reminded us regularly growing up that he didn't believe in giving his children money because it would take away their motivation. But this one time, he apparently did. (In my teens I once suggested he test his theory by doing an experiment with me as the one child who gets money—and my two sisters as the control group—and see how we do. "If I fail," I reasoned, "you'll at least have supporting data to back up your theory" But all I got was a laugh.)

As the story goes, I was eight years old at the time and totally oblivious to the fact that I had just become a millionaire. At least "on paper," as a lot of millionaires seem to be fond of saying. I'm not sure what that means, but I like the sound of it and so I'm repeating it here.

The irony is that very same year, my annual income (my allowance of $1.25) was only $65, albeit a $13 and 25% increase over the previous year's income. How did that happen? I had learned my father had a business windfall selling KFC and decided to leverage his recent good fortune as an opportunity to get an increase in my weekly allowance. I walked into his bathroom, where he was brushing his teeth while standing in his boxers. He told me something about how his mom had taught him to brush vertically rather than horizontally and he agreed that was the better brushing motion for good dental hygiene. But that's not what I was there to talk about, so I got right to the point, "Dad, is it true that after selling Kentucky Fried Chicken, you are a millionaire?"

My father paused, caught off guard, and as he wiped away the white toothpaste foam that had oozed out of the corner of his mouth, he cocked his head tentatively and said, "Hmm, you know Johnny, we might be." Then he reminded me that it was not nice to talk about money issues but wanted to know why I asked.

"Well Dad, I'm currently getting a dollar a week allowance. And I was wondering if now might be a good time to increase it to, say, $1.35" (I really was hoping for an increase to $1.25 but had learned from my father in negotiations you should ask for a little more than you actually want as a starting point, so I did).

My father paused and acted like he was running the numbers in his head to see if an extra 35 cents a week was doable under our new budget. He reluctantly yet confidently said he felt that was a reasonable request but that we should only bump it up to $1.25 for now and see how it goes.

I was ecstatic! I felt like I had just outmaneuvered my father, who was known nationally as a great negotiator, with my savvy tactic of asking for a weekly allowance of $1.35 while hoping to get just $1.25 and then getting it. I was on an adrenaline high and already looking for my next negotiation.

And the whole time, without even knowing it, I was sitting on a cool million -- in a trust in some bank somewhere. I was totally oblivious to my true temporary financial status -- unable to even enjoy complaining about all the taxes I was going to have to pay.

Looking back, what would I have done had I known? Hard to say. I probably blown most of it. I could easily see myself buying girls in my third grade class all the chocolate milk they could drink in hopes of getting them to chase me harder at recess.

I would have used another chunk to buy baseball cards, which I passionately collected that same year.

I would not have invested it well. When I had saved my $65 at the end of fiscal year '71 (52 weeks times $1.25), my mother took me to Louisville National Bank to open my first savings account. I spilled out the one dollar bills onto the desk of the branch manager. He told me I would get 3 or 4% interest in a savings account.

"What?!" I exclaimed. "That's only about $2 a year!" I collected my money, thanked the nice branch manager, and told him I felt I could do better keeping it in my room and using it to play pool with my neighborhood friends for a quarter a game— where I could certainly do better than $2 a year.

The next year, 1972, was a very bad year for me financially. My father decided to invest in a restaurant chain called Lums which was famous for selling beer-steamed hot dogs and to use the money from my sister's and my trusts to "make our money work for us." That's a way to talk about money that you don't want to put in a bank where it will only earn 3 or 4% annually. But it doesn't always work out. All that trust money was lost on the Lums investment and I was as broke at age nine as I had been at age seven. I've never been able to eat a beer-steamed hot dog since.

That's right, as big a year as 1971 was for me, 1972 was just as awful. In fact, it was devastating. Most kids in fourth grade gripe about having to learn geography or a foreign language or getting braces. Try losing a million dollars and then come cry on my shoulder about having to memorize foreign capitals or the awkwardness of eating an apple with braces on.

It's probably just as well I didn't know about the turn in my financial fortunes. I could have fallen into a major depression and this was before Prozac was on the scene to help us cope with life's cruel twists of fate. Third grade was tough enough for me without knowing. And, yes, I did get braces that year.

I'm glad I eventually learned about this whole exciting episode in my younger life and don't mind that I didn't know about it then.

Nowadays when I am worrying about getting bills paid, anticipating the next college tuition bill in the mail, or planning the next vacation we can't quite afford but are taking anyway because the memories will be worth it, I can remind myself of that year—now 41 years ago—when I was briefly, on paper, a real-life millionaire and didn't even know it. I can remind myself there was a brief time in my life when I could have easily afforded all these things and didn't have a financial worry in the world.

When I was eight years old.

TSA and Social Status

Today I tried, mistakenly, to enter the TSA pre-check security entrance at the airport but was waved away and told to go to the regular security line.

I apologized and got into the correct line, which was very long, and while I was waiting, I stared longingly at those walking briskly through the pre-check line.

The pre-check people seemed nice and generally happy and tried to avoid eye contact with their higher security risk brethren. They were better dressed and seemed more excited about where they were going and had an air of self-confidence lacking in the non-pre-check group.

I wondered if pre-check people were always this way or became this way after they got approved for TSA pre-check status.

I recognized one person in the TSA pre-check line I had lunch with recently. He said hello but was distant and I wondered if he felt it would be beneath him to have lunch with me again now that he knew I'm in a different flight security class than he and his family.

I did my best to appear like I wasn't trying to sneak weapons or sharp objects onto the plane and to give the impression that I knew how to act responsibly when flying. Most pre-check people didn't seem that concerned and were mostly just glad to be sectioned off from the rest of us and able to move quickly through the security line. One even looked compassionately at me after I caused the security buzzer to go off and I had to remove my belt and walk through the screening area again.

Sure, I made it through the second time, but it was clear to all around me I was in the right check in group.

And that's OK. I started to feel a camaraderie with non-pre-check people. A unique bond with my temporarily shoe-less and belt-less brothers and sisters. Perhaps these were "my people." We seemed to "get" each other on a deep but hard to define level.

We non-pre-checks are great in number and need to have each other's back.

On the flight, I was seated between a pre-check and non-pre-check person but only talked to the non-pre-check person. It was a loyalty thing. Besides, the pre-check person kept his earbuds in the entire flight and pretended to sleep so he wouldn't have to talk to us non-pre-checks. That is such a pre-check thing to do and, frankly, one more reason why I'm glad I'm not one of them.

Gifted with Emotional Intelligence

Rebecca and I were walking on Bardstown Road Sunday night looking for some place to eat. Rebecca was commenting about a friend of ours in Sunday school and how smart he seemed and asked me if I agreed.

"Yes, of course. You know, he once told me he thought I had high emotional intelligence, so obviously I think he has good judgment." I joked.

There was a pause.

"Don't you agree?" I asked Rebecca.

"I don't know. I've never really thought of you as someone who has really high emotional intelligence."

"What? Really? You don't think I have high emotional intelligence?"

"I really just don't know," Rebecca answered. "You sometimes have trouble remembering people's names who you should know."

"That's not a lack of emotional intelligence. That's a memory issue," I explained. "I can still size up a situation or have a sense of what makes someone tick without remembering their name."

"Oh, OK" Rebecca responded. "I guess I just can't imagine a person with high emotional intelligence arguing about how high their emotional intelligence is."

"Look," I explained. "Just because someone has high emotional intelligence doesn't mean they won't defend themselves when someone else suggests they're emotionally challenged"

"Whatever you say."

"It's not just my opinion," I corrected Rebecca. "I actually took a test for emotional intelligence online a few years ago and scored very high on it."

"Are you serious?" Rebecca asked, staring blankly at me.

"You know, I think I've lost my appetite," I said. "Let's just go home" We got in the car and drove home, largely in silence.

Although I don't text and drive, at stop lights I did search my phone to try to find the email with my emotional intelligence test score – but didn't want Rebecca to know that's what I was looking for.

After we got home, I finally found my online test score and proudly showed Rebecca.

Rebecca laughed. "It's a self-assessment test."

I started laughing, too, and said, "But I was being very objective with my answers. I promise."

Rebecca added, "If the kids and I took the test for you, we would have gotten a very different score"

We were both laughing now.

I said "Well, I just hope you've learned your lesson." "Oh, I definitely have." Rebecca jokingly conceded. "I'm sorry," I said. "I was being silly."

"Me, too" Rebecca chimed back. We hugged.

"I'm just glad there's still room for us to hug despite all the space my enormous emotional intelligence takes up," I joked.

We laughed again.

I thought to myself that perhaps being able to laugh at yourself after making a fool of yourself is a sign of emotional intelligence and validates my high self-assessed score. But decided someone who truly had a high emotional intelligence score wouldn't need to point that out.

The Perils and Power of Praying with your Partner

During a recent routine physical, my doctor found some concerning results in my blood work and asked me to come in for some follow-up tests, which indicated I needed to see a specialist for still further tests to rule out anything serious.

I felt like I would probably be OK but was concerned. That night after I told Rebecca about it, I asked if we could pray together and she said, "Yes. Of course."

I felt comforted by my wife joining me in prayer. I believe in the power of prayer and couldn't imagine anything but good coming from it.

Rebecca and I had done this before at the suggestion of a friend who told us praying together can be a great habit for couples and to avoid worrying about sounding eloquent and to stay focused on your own praying and not your partner's.

We knelt down, held hands and I prayed first. I asked God to please help me be free of the health problems that were concerning me and then added some "filler" prayer about other people and other things so it wouldn't seem to Rebecca and God like I wasn't being overly self-centered and praying only for myself.

Then it was Rebecca's turn. She asked God to please give her a "fuller heart" and then something else I couldn't quite make out. I asked her to repeat it. I figured if I couldn't hear it, God may not have been able to either. Rebecca again prayed for God give her a fuller heart and then followed with a more detailed way of saying what she had already said. Frankly, I didn't feel the second part of her prayer added much at all. But I was trying to focus on my praying and not Rebecca's.

We both said "Amen" and then stood up and hugged. As hard as I tried not to think about Rebecca's prayer, I couldn't help notice she never asked God for me to be free of any health problems. I figured it was just an oversight on her part. I couldn't imagine Rebecca purposely not praying for my health because she felt doing so would give up an important chit with God that she was saving for something more important. So I just let it go.

The next morning Rebecca and I got coffee and saw a good friend from church who had gone through some serious health challenges a few years ago and now was doing well. I shared with him my recent health concerns and he kindly assured me, "John, I'll be praying for you to get a good medical report." I made sure Rebecca was listening and responded, "Thank you. I'll be doing the exact same thing myself!" I paused and looked over at Rebecca to see if she had anything to add. But she didn't. Rebecca just smiled and hugged our friend goodbye and wished him a happy Derby weekend.

This was Rebecca's second prayer snub for me in 24 hours and was obviously much harder for me to dismiss as just an oversight on her part. I didn't say anything, but I was definitely bothered by it.

That night Rebecca and I were at dinner and she asked how I was doing. I told her I was a little anxious about the follow-up blood tests being done the next day and hoped everything was OK. I tried to resist saying anything more but couldn't. "Do you remember when we prayed   last night?"

"Sure." Rebecca answered lovingly.

"Well, I kinda noticed when we were praying that you didn't pray for me for my tests to come back clear."

"What? Yes, I did!" Rebecca shot back defensively.

"No. You really didn't. Because I was listening closely for it and it just didn't happen" I paused to let it sink in and added, "At first, I thought it was an oversight. But when you had a second chance to mention praying for me this morning at coffee and didn't take it, it bothered me."

Rebecca explained, "The reason I didn't ask God for your tests to be clear is because I have been taught only to pray for God's will to be done instead of asking for specific things that I want Him to do for me."

"What?" I responded incredulously. "You're saying you didn't pray for my health because of some new prayer orthodoxy you just learned?"

"Yes. I'm serious," Rebecca defended herself.

I sighed and shook my head. "I'm sorry. I just don't think I can buy that. If you were praying for our children—or even our dogs for that matter — I suspect you would ask God to 'please help them be in good health (or whatever you were wanting for them) and then maybe after that add, 'if it be Thy will.' But I can't see you just praying, 'Thy will be done' without offering God other suggestions if it involved our kids or our dogs."

Rebecca looked both perplexed and exasperated.

I continued, "Look, I'm not mad. I can't tell you how you should pray.

That's between you and God. All I know is that if you were the one having medical tests tomorrow, I would ask God for your tests to be clear"

"OK. OK. OK!" Rebecca interrupted. "I'll be sure to ask God for your tests to be clear the next time we pray."

"Don't do that." I said defensively. "I'm not even sure I want you now."
"What?" Rebecca blurted in confusion.

"I sure don't want you to pray for my health if it's just to make me feel better. I want you to really mean it."

"Of course, I'll mean it," Rebecca said. "I'm just not very eloquent at praying and wasn't thinking. I want nothing more than for you to be well. I just forgot to say it."

"Really?" I asked. "Do you mean that?" Rebecca assured me she did and

I began to feel better about things and changed our conversation to a lighter topic.

Later that night before bed, Rebecca and I knelt down again and held hands in prayer. Rebecca went first this time and asked God for a "fuller and more loving heart" but this time added, "And please help with John's health."

I have to admit I was a little disappointed. "Please help with John's health"? It seemed weak and vague to me—and unlikely to have much of an impact at all. But I didn't say anything. I was just glad Rebecca was trying. I bowed my heard and took my turn. I asked God to please help me to get "a clean bill of health with my medical tests" and before I could finish my prayer, Rebecca interrupted and added, "And please God help John to get a clean bill of health with his upcoming medical tests."

Rebecca nailed it that time. Sure, she was just repeating my prayer verbatim, but I felt like she finally "got it" and was fully on board with doing all she could, prayer-wise, to help me out.

We said, "Amen," and stood up, and I thanked Rebecca.

The next day at the doctor's office Rebecca and I held hands waiting for my results to come back. It was a long wait. I apologized to her for being silly about how she prayed for me. I told her I was scared and wanted all the help I could get. She kissed me on the forehead and I said, "Thank you for being here with me today. As always."

Rebecca said, "Of course. That's what I do. I'm always here for you and the kids. That's my life."

I smiled and said, "Well, I guess being there for the ones you love is about the most important job a person can have in this world." Rebecca kissed me again on the forehead and we continued to wait.

Eventually the doctor came in and told us that the new tests didn't indicate anything that we should be concerned about. It was a huge relief. There would be some follow-up tests, but I was essentially getting a clean bill of health. I hugged Rebecca tightly and thanked her for being such a good and supportive partner.

That night Rebecca and I knelt again to pray. We thanked God for all our blessings—with a special mention of my good test results. There were no special requests this time for either Rebecca or me. I was willing to pray for something for Rebecca if she wanted me to but she said she couldn't think of anything. I did throw in a special thanks to God for providing me with such a loving and supportive spouse. I felt like it was the least I could do.

Praying together as a couple is a very good thing, but not as simple as it sounds.

I know we aren't supposed to focus on each other's prayers, but Rebecca noticed my special thanks to God for her and thanked me afterwards.

There was nothing more I had wanted from Rebecca's prayer that night.

It felt really good, and I am already looking forward to praying together with Rebecca tomorrow night.

I secretly hoped Rebecca would thank God for giving her such a loving and supportive husband, but I decided I probably wasn't going to say anything if she didn't.

Cabela's

I've been needing to get something at Cabela's and decided to swing by recently. Cabela's is a national chain of hunting and camping megastores and kind of a 'guy's guy' store.

As I walked in an older gentleman working there was telling a story to a customer and squinted at me as if to say, "What are you doing here? Did you get lost on your way to Bed, Bath and Beyond?"

It's not the first time I've seen that look. I've gotten it before at Home Depot.

I looked down and noticed I was wearing suede loafers, so I couldn't blame him. I tried not to let his confounded glance bother me and began walking with a tougher and more self-assured stride --- like a guy who hunts and camps a lot --- as I also tried to remember where suede comes from.

I walked by the camouflage section then by a section selling deer and elk scents (for hunting, not cologne). There is aisle after aisle of every imaginable kind of hunting, camping and fishing equipment.

I was reminded of my younger days camping with my Uncle Jim Bob and my cousins in the Smoky Mountains of Tennessee. I was starting to like this place.

Then a female employee walked up to me and asked what I was looking for and if she could help.

I hesitated before sputtering, "Yes ma'am. Would you please tell me where I could find some, um (I cleared my throat), uh... pepper spray."

I paused awkwardly as she tried to conceal a slight grin. She seemed to suspect the only thing I'd ever hunted for was bargains.

I explained, "I gave my pepper spray to my daughter when she went to college and I just, you know, needed to get a replacement for..." my voice trailed off as I realized I was only making matters worse.

I tried to recover by clearing my throat again and squinting my eyes sternly in the direction she was pointing where I could find the pepper spray.

She couldn't have been nicer and asked me if I saw the African moose. I said I did (even though I have no idea what an African moose looks like and had to Google it on my phone). She told me the pepper spray was right behind that moose.

After several failed attempts at guessing the right moose, I found the pepper spray display and grabbed the largest bottle available and went to the checkout counter.

I selected the checkout aisle with an older gentleman, who I would describe as slightly rustic but possibly a closet metrosexual, and hoped he wouldn't judge me. He treated me like a regular guy who was making a typical run for pepper spray. No big deal. Just another Cabela guy.

And I have to admit, it feels good being a Cabela guy.

I strode to my car and got in. As I backed up, I nodded to the guy pulling in next to me and he nodded back. Another Cabela guy, just like me.

Sure, he was in an over-sized black pick-up truck that made my ride look like a toy car next to his. But I wasn't intimidated — not anymore, as I glanced at my large can of Fogger Jogger pepper spray and pulled confidently out of the Cabela's parking lot.

Teeth are the Window to our Soul

I started seeing a new dentist today.

We visited before my check-up and it turns out we know some of the same people and spent time in some of the same places when we were kids.

We seemed to hit it off and I think he felt like I was pretty solid guy.

And then he looked into my mouth for the first time. When he came up it was as if there was a sign on the back of my throat that said "This guy makes lots of bad dental choices and has been lying to dentists about flossing regularly for nearly five decades. Don't trust him."

I wanted to explain but didn't want my new dentist to know I knew what he was thinking.

So instead I changed the subject to something more upbeat: What was the best toothpaste for sensitive teeth. And, yes, I sucked up big time by asking his assistant for a recommendation for the strongest dental floss available as I tried to create the impression that I had, in fact, always been a serious flossers who simply needed better guidance and stronger floss.

When I left we shook hands and I felt I had rehabilitated myself in his eyes—but only partially. Fortunately, he didn't base his entire opinion of me on my lowly right third molar. He realized there was more to me than that one poorly cared for tooth and it was just one of 31 total teeth in my mouth. (I had a wisdom tooth extracted last year due, in part, to negligent dental hygiene. But there were mitigating circumstances that are too complicated to rehash here). My other 30 teeth weren't necessarily impressively maintained–a basis for trust and respect with my new dentist—but at least they were good enough to buy me a second chance to make a better first impression.

It's too bad because I felt I had my new dentist at "Hello. I really needed to get my teeth cleaned today and am glad you could fit me in." But then I had to go and open my mouth and let him look inside. That's where things went all wrong and I now wish I had been more reserved and selective about the teeth I showed him on my first visit.

It's important to remember that for most people you meet for the first time, they view our eyes as the windows to our soul. But with dentists, it is several inches below and only after you open wide. Our teeth, viewed in this way, are a kind of Rosetta Stone of who we really are as a person. Are we responsible? Do we have our priorities right? Do we plan ahead? Do we do daily maintenance work for things we are supposed to? Can we be trusted with the health and welfare of 32 permanent adult teeth? If not, what does that say about us in other areas of our lives?

Let's not forget that no matter how good we pretend to be on the outside, a dentist peering into a new patient's mouth is like a seasoned and street smart pastor who has seen it all staring into our flawed, and unflossed souls.

We hope when meeting a new person that they will see us as we want to be seen. But when that new person is a dentist that hope is short-lived. As soon as the dentist comes up from glancing into our mouths that first time, they no longer see us as we want to be seen but as we really are, cavities, crowns, gingivitis and all.

My Emergency Room Experience

I checked into an emergency room last Saturday evening in North Carolina with agonizing back pain and nausea and was immediately diagnosed with kidney stones and injected with anti-nausea and anti-pain meds and placed in a waiting area.

I was grateful for the pain relief and sat in a numbed stupor with my wife as we waited for x-rays. I hadn't eaten since morning and asked Rebecca if she would get me some cookies from the vending machine and she did, a yellow package of two Grandma's Homestyle peanut butter cookies. I was thrilled and started to open them when my nurse darted around the corner and pointed her finger at me and said sharply, "You can't eat anything until the doctor does your scans, OK? No cookies."

I grimaced and tossed the packet of cookies on the table next to me but kept them within my line of vision and reach.

Rebecca said, "Oh well. Guess you can't eat anything yet."

Rebecca left to meet our daughter for a concert we were all supposed to attend and said she would be back as soon as it was over.

I sat alone glumly staring at the TV which was playing a show on the Food Network about child chefs competing to make the best dessert.

None of their desserts looked very good to me but I kept gazing at the packet of Grandma's Homestyle cookies just a few inches away. My favorite kind, too, peanut butter.

I waited to make sure the nurse wasn't watching and slyly opened the packet and ate one-fourth of one cookie. And then another fourth. I was about to eat a third fourth but heard someone coming and quickly crumpled the cookie package and stuffed it in my pants pocket and stared listlessly at the TV.

A few minutes later my nurse was back with a wheelchair to take me to a new waiting area. As I began to stand up, several cookie crumbs tumbled down my sweater and one tiny yellow crumb stayed stuck on me like Velcro.

I didn't brush them off because I didn't want to call attention to them.

I closed my eyes waiting for the nurse to scold me but she said nothing

For a split second I thought to myself, "If she says anything about the cookie crumbs, just act like you don't know how they got there." I felt guilty having that thought but she intimidated me and I didn't want her mad at me in the condition I was in.

Fortunately, it never came up and I figured I just got lucky and she didn't notice.

She dropped me off in a new waiting area but said absolutely nothing to me all the way there and even after dropping me off.

I waited and waited and waited. The pain and anti-nausea meds were wearing off. I began sweating and feeling faint as the back pain and nausea returned.

I splashed water on my face and groaned audibly hoping someone would help.

About two hours in, I staggered up to the nurses station and asked how much longer it would be and was told they weren't sure.

A little later, my nurse walked by and I tried to look especially pitiful and hoped she had some news but she kept walking and didn't even make eye contact with me.

I waited in the hallway for her to return and when she did I told her in a faint whispy voice that I was embellishing for effect that my pain and anti-nausea meds had worn off and asked her if she could help.

She looked at me like someone who was holding ticket #73 at the car wash and said, "We are doing all we can and it shouldn't be a lot longer before the doctor can see you."

I fell back in my wheel chair and started making a groaning noise that was just loud enough to be heard at the nurses station around the corner. I groaned increasingly louder for the next 15 minutes.

Finally, I saw my nurse coming again and figured my plan had worked. She stopped and turned to me then said, "The people who you hope will hear you, can't hear you" and then walked off.

"Is this about the cookies!?" I thought to myself.

I was stunned and furious and helpless all at the same time.

I couldn't take back the half cookie I ate two hours ago and couldn't get her to feel sorry for me after ignoring her order.

But I did think of something I could do -- and did it. I dug deep into my pants pocket and pulled out the remaining smooshed Grandma's Homestyle peanut butter cookie and ate it slowly and messily allowing crumbs to fall all over my sweater and not brushing them off. I placed the crumpled bright yellow Grandma's Homestyle cookie packet on the chair right beside me for all to see.

I felt better - quite a bit better, as a matter of fact -- for several minutes. Then the pain returned.

Two hours later, I was told they were ready to do my scans but my kidney stone had already passed -- and my nurse never even saw the empty cookie package.

Maybe they really were that busy. Maybe there were many more patients much sicker than I who needed urgent care that night. I can't say for sure

But if you are ever in an emergency room in North Carolina and told not to eat cookies, do yourself a favor and do as you're told.

45

Best Deal on a Watch Anywhere

Last summer Maggie, Rebecca and I were attending a play in New York on a Sunday afternoon and the lights went up and the audience began applauding and I stood up to clap, in part because it was a great play and partly because it was finally over, but it wasn't. The couple behind us explained it was the second intermission. I looked at Maggie hoping she was as restless as I was and ready to leave early and thrilled when she indicated she was. Rebecca insisted on staying but didn't mind if we left so Maggie could buy a pair of jeans she'd been wanting and we agreed to meet in an hour and a half at 5:30 in Times Square.

Maggie and I darted out of the theater relieved and headed to the first department store we could find and she tried on jeans while I meandered over to the men's watch section to look for a watch for myself. I had gotten a name from a friend of a watch dealer in the Diamond District who he promised would give me "the best deal on a watch anywhere" and I was hoping if I bought Maggie the jeans she wanted she would agree to let me go to the Diamond District to see this watch dealer.

Maggie slipped up behind me with her bag in hand and asked facetiously, "Are you looking for a watch for mom?"

"Um, well, not just yet. But I could, though." I replied weakly.

"You know Mom has been wanting a watch for a long time?" Maggie reminded me.

"I know." I agreed. I wasn't thrilled with this development because I was really planning on getting a watch for myself but I played along hoping Maggie would let it go.

But Maggie has a habit of not letting things go and of finishing what she starts.

"When was the last time you got Mom a gift that wasn't for her birthday or Christmas -- the last time you got her a gift without a reason?"

There was a pause. "What?" I mumbled.

Maggie repeated the question.

"Well, I would say probably it was about…uh…"

Maggie raised her eyebrow as I fumbled for an answer.

"I would say that it is probably about that time again --to get Mom a present without having a reason." I smiled pleased with myself that I had finagled an answer that Maggie liked.

We had less than an hour left before stores closed so we went to the women's watch section in the department store but they didn't have anything that caught our eye. We left for another department store and Maggie began describing the exact kind of watch Rebecca wanted. She wanted a watch with a gold and silver toned bracelet and blue face. The second department store didn't have what we were looking for either.

I suggested the Diamond District and the name my friend had given me and Maggie agreed. We hailed a cab and headed there but they were closed on Sunday. There was still about 30 minutes left before stores closed. We dashed into a vintage watch shop and found a watch that fit Rebecca's description but it was old –about 50 years old. I was tempted and we were running out of time. Maggie thought maybe we should buy it, too. It was even in the price range we had decided on. But I noticed the second hand wasn't moving. I asked the salesperson about it and he shook the watch hard. Still no movement. He shook it harder several more times and finally the second hand began moving. But it just didn't seem like the right decision. We didn't want to get Rebecca a nice watch that only worked sporadically.

There were two more watch stores nearby that closed in 20 minutes and we grabbed a taxi and sped to the first. We ran in breathless and looked hopefully but, again, nothing quite right. We headed to the second and final store before we would meet up with Rebecca. This store had to be the one. We strode in 5 minutes before it closed. The salesperson tried to help us but the watch we were looking for was too specific and just wasn't there.

As we walked out they locked the door behind us and we headed toward Times Square feeling defeated. But the Internet is a wonderful thing in times like these. I Googled the watch description and the watch, exactly as Rebecca had described it, popped up for sale in a store in California. I showed Maggie and she nodded enthusiastically but the price was nearly double what we were expecting and had agreed on. We were now in Times Square and Rebecca would be there any minute. I searched furiously online for a better deal for a similar watch but kept coming back to the first one -- the one I felt I couldn't afford. It was 5:30 and we could see Rebecca walking toward us. I clicked purchase and began furtively typing in the credit card information as Rebecca approached and began telling us how we had missed a great ending to the play and asked if we would take a picture together in Times Square using the camera extension pole she brought with her.

Maggie knew I was completing the purchase so she tried stalling Rebecca who was getting frustrated with us and was already mildly irritated that we didn't stay for the entire play. I gave Maggie the OK to let her know I completed the purchase and we both were smiling mischievously as Rebecca was gently scolding us for not posing for a picture. Rebecca suspected we were up to something but had no idea what it was.

"What are you all laughing about?" Rebecca asked suspiciously.

I turned my phone around and showed Rebecca an enlarged picture of the watch we just bought for her and said, "We thought you might like this and just got it for you. It will be waiting for you when we get home."

Rebecca was overwhelmed and teared up instantly. "I don't understand what's happening. Why did you all do this?"

"We just wanted to and because you deserve it and have been wanting this for a long time." I answered.

Rebecca was crying and leaned over to hug Maggie who stopped her and pointed to me and said, "It was Dad's idea." That made me tear up as Rebecca hugged me first and then hugged Maggie. And as Maggie watched both Rebecca and me teary-eyed, she teared up too. There we were, the three of us, in Times Square, on a Sunday afternoon, laughing together and wiping away tears of joy.

It was the best deal on a watch anywhere.

Just Another Sunday Afternoon

It was just another Sunday afternoon. The Kansas City Chiefs were playing the Green Bay Packers on TV.

My father was playing cards with some friends, probably gin rummy. My mom was hosting and I was just kind of hanging around and   I remember getting one of the men to play basketball with me earlier in the day. We had a basketball goal in the driveway but not much room to play. So we just shot around instead of playing HORSE or one-on-one. In the back we had a kidney-shaped pool and area for grilling out. It was on the beach and I loved staying there because at nighttime I could hear the ocean waves crash rhythmically against the sand until I fell asleep.

But this was a Sunday afternoon and I was bored amidst all the activity. Not much for an eight-year-old to do. Mostly adult fun. I walked out back and looked at the beach. An older lady in a bathing suit wrapped in a towel seemed anxious and waved to me.. She had long gray hair and large sunglasses, and she asked if I'd seen a young child wandering on the beach. She described the child, but I was only half- listening. She told me that she had fallen asleep on the beach watching her grandchild and just woke up. A man from the party walked up to us and listened as she explained again what had happened.

Suddenly, I had something to do. Like a game, almost. My job was to find this wandering child before anyone else did. I walked up and down the beach but didn't see any young children. The older man from my parent's party acted like he was looking too but he really wasn't. He stood by the grill area and craned his neck a little and used his hand to block the sun from his eyes to get a better view. But he saw no children either.

I felt for the grandmother but was also getting a little annoyed she wanted me and not an adult to help her out. I walked around to the front of the house and saw nothing. It was getting windy and a little chilly, and I wandered back to where I had seen the grandmother originally and she wasn't there. I figured she left. I went back toward the house but stepped toward the pool and walked alongside the curve where the pool was shaped like the turned-in side of a kidney. My job every morning was to take a long pole and skim the pool of any debris that had collected from the day before. I was imagining doing that as I walked toward the deep end where I suddenly saw a child-like blur languishing at the pool bottom. I dashed inside and screamed to my father that a baby was in the bottom of the pool. My dad leapt out of his chair where he was playing cards, knocking it over as he ran outside and in seemingly one motion and dove straight into the deep end pulling out the baby. He had been a competitive swimmer growing up and got to the baby faster than anyone else there could have.

My mother called 911 and it seemed the paramedics were there instantaneously. My mother seemed calmer than she was as tears welled in her eyes as she led the paramedics to the baby. I was kept on the other side of the pool, away from all the activity. I remember hearing that they turned the baby upside down and water came flushing out of its tiny body. But it was too late. The baby had been underwater for too long and had drowned and couldn't be resuscitated.

I don't remember much after that. It was a horrifying shock that wasn't supposed to happen on a Sunday afternoon when parents are socializing with friends and kids are bored and it's too chilly to be on the beach and the Kansas City Chiefs and Green Bay Packers are playing a football game that everyone seems interested in. And a baby wanders off from a sleeping grandmother on the beach outside and falls into your pool and drowns and the whole world turns upside down and your life is changed forever. On just another Sunday afternoon.

And the waves at night never again sound as soothing as they crash rhythmically against the sand as you try to fall asleep.

A New Year's Resolve

"Death is most tragic when it surprises us in the midst of our hopes."

That was the first sentence of the obituary I wrote for my friend Bruce Fellman, who died tragically 35 years ago while we were on a college semester abroad.

Bruce had become my closest friend among the 500 students from universities and colleges across the country to travel around the world and learn about different cultures. Bruce was the editor of the school newspaper and encouraged me to write for it and I did. I never expected to write his obituary a few months later.

I don't remember the specifics of what I wrote after that first sentence but it was basically describing Bruce's charisma and charm, his enthusiasm for life, his quirkiness and creativity, and his adventurous desire to experience new things. The last trait in particular was something I lacked and drew me to Bruce. In many ways he was my alter-ego – he possessed qualities I wished I had and I hoped being friends with him might cause them to rub off on me.

Bruce and I travelled together in each port for two and a half months discovering the world and ourselves in the process. Bruce was from Nebraska and attended American University where he was majoring in journalism but felt he would most likely end up in business, either as an entrepreneur or working in commercial real estate with his step-father, who he admired and cared for deeply. Bruce was extremely close to his mother and shared stories about her as well as his group of close-knit friends back home.

As fun-loving and zestful about life as Bruce was, he also had a strong sense of himself and was practical and realistic. We did what many ambitious college students do: spending evenings drinking and debating the meaning of life, theology and politics, except I took these conversations too much to heart while Bruce had the wisdom not to take life or himself too seriously.

When we got to Sri Lanka, Bruce and I travelled with a different group of friends for the first time. It was a beautiful and mystical country but when our group returned to the ship a few days later, we were told one student hadn't returned and may have been in an accident and possibly died. I overheard someone say it was Bruce Fellman and remember stumbling as I ran to find a senior administrator to tell me if it was. A professor pulled me aside and confirmed it was Bruce. I emotionally cratered and went to my room throwing the ladder from my bunk bed across the room and pounding the walls with my fists and crying alone for several hours. When I opened my cabin door, Barry Paris, Bruce's and my journalism professor, had left a note at the foot of my door with a poem from the Greek poet Aeschylus, "Sorrow falls on the heart, drop by drop, until finally, by the awful grace of God, comes wisdom."

I'd never experienced death close up. I'd never imagined someone my own age could die. I couldn't believe someone who was my dear friend and who I looked up to and wanted to be like, could be gone so quickly and tragically.

Bruce's parents reached out to me and I didn't respond. They ran into my parents in Washington, DC a year later and asked if they would encourage me to contact them but I didn't. I was depressed and despondent and didn't know what to say to parents who just lost their son. I felt terrible for not responding, but wasn't strong enough to know what to do, so I did nothing.

Years passed. Two decades passed.

I was 41 years old and we had just moved and I was going through boxes of old items and found pictures of Bruce from the semester 20 years earlier. I thought about reaching out to his family after all those years but knew that would be too awkward.

A few nights later I couldn't sleep and was watching a foreign movie with English subtitles about a young family who lost their teenage son. Something in that movie --the sympathizing with the parents -- gave me the courage to write Bruce's mom a long letter apologizing for not responding to her 20 years earlier and saying to her all the things I wished I had said then. I told her how much Bruce had meant to me and how grateful I was for our friendship and that even though Bruce had died far too young, his spirit and memory were still alive in all whose lives he'd touched, including mine in Louisville, Kentucky.

A week later I received a letter back from Bruce's mom thrilled to have heard from me and explaining they have an annual celebration for Bruce's life with his closest friends and inviting me to join them the following Saturday for the 20 year anniversary of Bruce's death. I couldn't financially afford to make a trip like that on such short notice but was wise enough to know I couldn't personally afford not to. An invitation like that wasn't an ordinary invitation or coincidence but something far more important -- even Providential – that I had to say yes to. I bought my plane ticket and a few days later was on a flight to Colorado, where Bruce's parents had moved.

I took a cab to their home. It was a large daunting door and I took a deep breath and knocked. A small lovely and effervescent woman answered, Bruce's mom, Darylynn. She hugged me as though we'd been friends for decades. She welcomed me inside and introduced me to Bruce's closest childhood friends –remarkable men who all had established careers but made time each year to celebrate their friend's life and the importance of their friendship.

Tom Fellman, Bruce's step-father, gave me a tour of downstairs and pointed to a picture of Bruce and began telling a story about him as his voice cracked and he began to cry and hugged me. He said he was so glad I came. I began crying too as I hugged him back.

We had dinner and told stories and laughed and joked and cried and laughed and talked some more. It was 3am before we finally called it a night. I hugged everyone goodbye and went back to my hotel room and was on my flight back home by 6am.

I stayed in touch with the Fellmans for the next several years and still stay in touch with several of Bruce's friends who are scattered across the country.

It was an experience I was afraid to attempt and one that would have been easy to ignore but I'm glad I didn't. It turned out to be one of the most rewarding experiences of my life.

And so, I wish for this new year, for myself and others, to find the courage to reach out to someone you've wanted to but haven't because you worried it would be too awkward.

The experience of laughing and crying with strangers who should be friends will ensure a year you will fondly remember and never regret.

The Existential Significance of Bathroom Art

A picture of a yellow bird hangs on our bathroom wall. I can't say I love it but it's adequate. It wasn't originally intended for our bathroom. I bought it on sale and in a hurry to fill up empty wall space in another room but now it hangs prominently on our bathroom wall instead. It's part of my life's daily scenery and will probably stay that way. It's "good enough" and has grown on me over time and now seems to fit there.

Which made me wonder how many other facets of my daily live are what they are simply because they are "good enough." Each day we have limited time to make unlimited life decisions --small, medium and large— and these cumulative daily life decisions add up over time to become the sum total of what and who we are.

I look at another wall in our bathroom and see two pictures of our family hanging there. The top picture is slightly crooked and probably has been since we hung it when we moved in nearly 5 years. But you can barely notice the slant and they are good enough just how they are and will stay there.

I look at our shower curtain next and it is pleasant looking and adequate, as shower curtains go. I can't remember who decided on the shower curtain. But it, too, is good enough and seems here to stay.

On our bathtub rim is the same brand of soap we have used for over 20 years. Buying soap hasn't been a conscious decision in our lives for two decades. Either my mother or mother-in-law recommended the brand of soap and it has been a fixture in our home ever since. That brand of soap didn't have to become a fixture, of course. But it did because, like so many other things in our lives, it's good enough.

As I continue my observational journey I catch my reflection in the bathroom mirror. I stop and see myself and ask if I am who I am because the habits, personal qualities and attitudes I have chosen for myself were chosen because they were "good enough." And wonder if these habits, personal qualities and attitudes that make me who I am today somehow managed to grow on me over time and now just seem to fit, like the picture of the yellow bird seems to fit on our bathroom wall?

I stare deeper into the mirror looking at myself looking at myself and don't want to answer that question. The question of whether I'm merely an accumulation of life decisions that just seemed "good enough" at the time but were never given adequate thought and made too quickly.

Instead of answering that question I choose to look back at the picture of the yellow bird to distract myself. And decide, for the moment, that I regret not trying harder to pick out a better wall hanging to fill up the empty space on our bathroom wall.

And hope my deflective response to the more poignant question I asked my reflection in the mirror is good enough.

What does Walgreens Know About me That I Don't Know?

I love Walgreens. Don't get me wrong.

But the "Be well" mantra from every Walgreens employee at the end of each verbal exchange is making me more than a little paranoid. It has me wondering what's wrong with me that Walgreen employees know about that I don't. .

I went to Walgreens today to buy some vitamins and toiletries. The sales clerk who helped me was very pleasant and as I walked away she said added, "Be well." I took it as a kind of encouraging "atta boy." It seemed like a natural—if somewhat meddlesome—thing to say.

After all, she had helped me find vitamins that will make me healthier, or "weller" in the Walgreens parlance.

But before leaving Walgreens I looked at some phone chargers and the sales clerk who helped me told me that they didn't carry what I was looking for. I thanked him and he, too, told me to "Be well." He said it in a more concerned tone and almost knowing manner. I thought that was odd and, frankly, it bothered me a little. I don't know him personally and I was just looking for a phone charger—not something that affected my health. Had he talked to the sales clerk who helped me with the vitamins section? Did he know I was taking a vitamin supplement because I worried my diet wasn't sufficient? Or was he just repeating a catchphrase he was told to say to every customer and was only pretending to be concerned about my health and, presumably, my phone charger situation?

As I walked to the checkout counter I wondered if Walgreens had somehow gotten involved with the Church of Scientology. I remember meeting some members of the Church of Scientology years ago and they seemed "programmed" and had certain buzzwords they used as they encouraged me to do a personal "audit" within the Dianetics program. Interacting with Walgreens employees is always pleasant. In fact, it's a little too pleasant. Almost robotic. And every conversation ends with the same mechanical "Be well" farewell and hope that my health will somehow improve. But it isn't clear what they are really saying to me. Do they know something about my health failing that I am not aware of? Or maybe Walgreens employees are using this hypnotic "Be well" chant to "guide me" to a better level of "being" within the Dianetics framework of personal growth.

I thought to myself I could easily see Tom Cruise and John Travolta shopping at Walgreens instead of Rite Aid. Why didn't this occur to me earlier?

As I checked out and tried to pay the sales clerk, he asked me if I was a "Balance Rewards Member." I said I didn't know what that meant. I figured it must be one of the levels of Scientology, but I didn't say anything. I gave the sales clerk my phone number as requested and he told me I was at the "Balance Rewards" level. As I watched him type in my phone number, I imagined all sorts of data about me was processing before his eyes.

I was informed I had reached a level of 27,000 points. I couldn't tell if that was good news for me—or if perhaps it meant my health was in jeopardy. As I took my bag and walked away, the cashier, who was a thoughtful and quiet man, kept staring at the floor and muttered to me almost against his will to "Be well."

Obviously he didn't mean it and was saying it merely as part of some Scientology "groupspeak." Based on all the information he had on me, I think he knew I wasn't going to make it. I turned back to him and motioned toward the vitamins I had purchased. I wanted him to know I was at least trying. But he said nothing. Not even "Be well" again. Just silence. What else could I conclude except he knew I didn't have much time left and that he was just trying to let me down easy by not being more direct and specific?

I left Walgreens with my vitamins and toiletries. But when I got home I felt like it was pointless to even start taking the vitamins. My fate was sealed and, based on my interactions with Walgreens employees, I figured it was time for me to get my affairs in order.

Who knew that the Walgreens employees and their creepy and overly solicitous "Be well" comments would convince me to update my will and to start making peace with the fact that my days are numbered? I just needed a multi-vitamin and some basic toiletries.

I wonder if I should try shopping at CVS for a second opinion?

As a Man Thinketh to Himself

My wife Rebecca is at work today at her new job and I'm home looking outside at the snow covering our driveway and began thinking to myself...

"Maybe I should clear the snow off the driveway?

Actually, it's going to get warmer in a few days and that will melt the snow, so I don't need to do that.

The only benefit to clearing the snow off the driveway today would be to impress Rebecca.

Do I want to impress Rebecca today? And if so, how much?

Are there other, less physically exhausting ways, to impress Rebecca?

Maybe I'll take her to dinner somewhere nice tonight to impress her instead of shoveling snow off our driveway.

Hmmm. But a nice dinner could get expensive and there's really not much snow out there. Maybe I should clear the driveway to impress her."

So, I go looking for the snow shovel in our garage but can't find it anywhere and think to myself:

"This is great. The best possible outcome, really. I can tell Rebecca I was going to shovel the driveway but couldn't find the shovel.

No, wait! She'll probably just tell me where it is from when she used it to shovel part of the driveway on Friday when I was out of town and that would be really embarrassing.

Or would it? Yes, it would.

Maybe I could buy a new snow shovel to impress Rebecca and not have to embarrass myself by asking her where the old one is.

But could I impress Rebecca by just BUYING a new snow shovel but NOT actually using it to shovel snow today? I could say, I'll shovel the driveway if it snows some more but it's really not bad enough yet and will probably melt away on its own in a day or two.

No, Rebecca will just get mad that I wasted money buying a new snow shovel we don't need and not even using it.

I wonder what restaurants are open tonight?"

Sometimes a Man's Gotta do What a Man's Gotta Do

Rebecca is out of town this week with our daughter. I miss them a lot but being home alone the past few days has reminded me that I really am the man of the house and it made me want to assert myself more at home.

A couple of weeks ago, Rebecca and I got into a squabble because I tried to replace a wall hanging in our bathroom that I don't care for and Rebecca reminded me that home decorating is not within the scope of my household duties. We tried that once about 18 years ago when Rebecca was pregnant with Maggie and I brought home a pink and black rug for our entrance hall and excitedly told Rebecca that I got it for a steal at a carpet store that was "going out of business."

Rebecca explained that that particular carpet store is always "going out of business" and my choice of colors was making her more nauseous than her morning sickness.

But being alone this week has emboldened me. I thought to myself, "This is my house, too. I even paid for it. And by golly, if I want to change one little wall hanging in our bathroom, I need to be man enough to just do it!"

So, I did.

Saturday afternoon I found a store having a sale and bought a wall hanging I liked and took down the wall hanging I don't like and put up my new one.

It felt good. It felt right. Like the universe is where it should be. It's a guy thing. Like grilling out steaks or hunting. It's hard to explain but sometimes us guys just need to be in charge.

I've looked at the new wall-hanging several times and feel very pleased with both my choice of artwork and my newfound boldness.

But tonight I remembered that Rebecca gets home tomorrow and I started nervously looking for the old picture to put back up and hope I can get my money back for the one I bought.

I never said manly assertiveness needed to last longer than a week. I just hope Rebecca doesn't notice.

Black Tie Stylin' and Improvisin'

Last night Rebecca and I went to a black-tie gala. It's a wonderful event but can be intimidating.

I needed to be downtown on business just prior to the gala so I put my tux in the car and took it out to change when I was done and rushed to the event. I was already late as I sat down at our table with a very elegant group of people and tried to blend in as smoothly as possible as dinner was being served.

As I scanned the other men around the dinner tables, I noticed they all had a pocket square in their tux's breast pocket. But I did not.

I got that awful sinking feeling that I had no business at this fancy affair and needed to do something quickly to fix it.

I looked down at my lap and noticed a bright white napkin. I started folding it and thought it might work perfectly as a pocket square. It was thick –a lot more material than a typical pocket square. I considered trying to rip it in half and then fold it but it was such a nice dinner napkin that I decided doing so would be terribly rude.

So, I just folded the napkin over several times, pressed it tightly, waited until no one was looking, and stuck it in my breast pocket.

I then tried to re-join the table conversation and eat my dinner. But when I needed to wipe my mouth, I remembered that my napkin was now in my breast pocket. I looked over at Rebecca's lap and thought I could borrow her napkin but I couldn't see it. She was engrossed in conversation with the woman sitting on the other side of me and I didn't want to interrupt. I again waited until no one was looking and snapped my pocket square/napkin out of my breast pocket and wiped my face.

Later, after I had finished eating, I re-folded my napkin and re- inserted it into my breast pocket with the clean end up. This time, though, I got a better look at it and instead of appearing to have a passable pocket square, I simply looked like a guy who gotten confused and mistakenly placed a large dinner napkin into his breast pocket.

My plan just wasn't working..

Since I'd already missed out on dinner conversation and struggled to enjoy eating my mostly napkin-less dinner, I gave up.

And, of course, no one cared or noticed, reminding me again the important life lesson that it is more important to be comfortable with yourself than fretting about fitting in.

And I was really glad I don't have an oversized napkin in our laundry basket the next morning.

Whole Foods Fraud Alert

I am not a regular shopper at Whole Foods Market.

I like going there, and I feel better about myself when I do. But it strikes me as a sort of community for its regular shoppers, who are often health conscious and committed to a lifestyle replete with vegan dieters and yoga instructors.

I just don't feel like I fit in there, and I suspect they sense I'm a fraud. Or at least a Kroger shopper who missed the turn for Kroger and was too lazy to turn around.

It's a little confusing for me and a little daunting too.

I experience the same sensation when I am at a hardware store. Just by looking at my hands, you can tell I have never been asked by a neighbor if they could borrow some of my tools. That would be pointless and embarrassing to me. Like asking the neighbor whose house is in foreclosure if you can borrow $20. Just a common-sense thing it never occurs to anyone to ask me in any neighborhood I have ever lived in.

So, bracing myself with my insecurities. I confidently strode into Whole Foods Market.

So far, so good. No one seems to be whispering "Who is that man who looks like he still buys Wonder Bread, and what's he doing here?"

I tried to look healthy and fit in. I mussed my hair and looked earnestly at a magazine featuring simple and austere living practices.

I noticed a lot of unhealthy looking people shopping and I wasn't sure if they were there to change the way they look or if their pallid complexions were the result of too many glasses of strained carrot juice.

I picked out a low-calorie dinner that I would love to have someone I know walk by me and see me eating and say, "John, I didn't know you were into Whole Foods" I could smile while chewing (healthy food is really easy to chew) and give them an affirming nod that says, "Oh yeah. I'm a regular" while not having to actually say it, since that would be a lie.

Nobody I knew saw me and now it was time to leave.

I put a serious concentrated look on my face with just a hint of deprivation that sent the message, "I may have just eaten, but I am nowhere near full." In other words, I was fitting in.

Until I walked out the store exit and, while standing in the alcove, bent down to look at the free magazine section. After thumbing through a publication with pictures of the health food culture equivalent of really, really smart looking people. Except instead of having a stratospheric IQ or two PhD's from MIT, they were just really fanatical about health food. And remote from me.

So I looked around to make sure no one was looking, and I grabbed the gigantic glossy and gaudy issue of Nfocus social magazine and quickly folded it under my arm and walked rapidly to my car --hoping to escape before the Whole Foods fraud alarm went off.

Letting Go of Slights

Thirty-one years ago, Rebecca and I had been dating for about six months and were browsing in a bookstore in Lexington and found a book that mentioned my father. It profiled his childhood and early business successes and ascribed part of his success to having "inexhaustible energy."

As I put the book back on the shelf I asked Rebecca if she felt I had inexhaustible energy and she said, "I don't see that in you."

Rebecca's comment wounded me and I insisted I really did have inexhaustible energy like my father, but that mine was more subtle and she just wasn't able to easily see and appreciate it. Rebecca offered some recent counter examples of me not having excessive energy and said we'd just have to agree to disagree.

We went back and forth for another 10 minutes until I left the bookstore in a huff and we barely spoke for the rest of the afternoon.

It was one of our early big arguments, as absurd as it was and as wildly over-sensitive as I was being, but we didn't bring it up again and just agreed to disagree.

Last night as Rebecca and I were watching television in bed and she was struggling to stay awake, she asked what time I was getting up and I reminded her I have my 6am men's group that I've been attending on Saturdays for the past several months.

Rebecca muttered sleepily, "I don't know how you do it."

I said softly, "Well, I have inexhaustible energy." After a pause, I added in an almost whisper, "I told you I did."

Rebecca may have already fallen asleep. I just don't know for sure. But I do know she didn't disagree this time and it felt really good.

Life from the Back Seat

I am writing this entreaty from the back seat of my wife's minivan. My daughter is sitting in the front seat and controlling the music and music volume (keeping it turned up just slightly higher than she knows I want it to be) and my wife is driving and the two of them are chatting away somehow over the music and seem to be laughing and enjoying each other's company.

I, as always, am alone in the back seat. I feel like a refugee from another country who can't speak the language and who doesn't understand the cultural customs.

I sometimes feel the loud music is to keep me muted. I can't engage in the conversation anyway because either 1) I can't hear well enough to understand it, 2) I don't understand it even when I can hear it, or 3) I make really "stupid" comments even when I can hear and understand what is being said.

I am worried it won't be long until I am asked to move to the trunk part of the minivan when we go out to eat—the part behind the final row of seats and the rear hatch. It is really cold back there in the winter and even lonelier than where I am sitting now. But only by a little. Although I suspect, on the positive side, the music won't seem as loud.

I am writing because I, frankly, don't know how this situation happened. It wasn't long ago that I confidently strode to the front passenger seat every time my wife drove the family out to eat. And I didn't even have to run to get to the front seat before anyone else.

At first it was an inconvenience but it was still clear (to me, at least) who was the head of the household. But it wasn't long before that sinking confidence turned into spiraling self-doubt and then eventually to the current state of near obsolescence.

I've tried to turn things around by playing to my current strengths and being even more annoying than usual but that didn't work I thought about offering to drive but I have a smallish compact car that the family never wants to drive anywhere.

I'm now out of plans to reassert myself to a position in my family, not of dominance, but simply relevance. I am much more realistic now. I don't even have to actually matte just as long as family members would be willing to pretend that I "could matter."

Is that asking too much? Or should I start dressing more warmly and placing pillows around the flooring and sides between the hatch and back seats, where I seem destined to find myself any night in the near future when we go out for family dinner?

Christmas Present Explanation

When our son was five years old, we surprised him Christmas morning with a new puppy. He was ecstatic but as he held the new puppy my wife and I noticed the puppy was shivering.

My wife commented to me several times about the shivering asking me if I thought it was normal and if our new puppy would be alright.

Finally, our commonsense 5-year-old son, Johnny, interrupted and said, "Mom, relax. The puppy has been on a sleigh all night long in cold weather. Of course she's going to be shivering."

What Overzealous Hyper-Competitive Parents Look Like

I used to make fun of overzealous hyper-competitive parents and vowed never to be one.

When my son was in kindergarten, his school had a tradition of a stick horse derby race. Parents take it seriously –very seriously. There were rumors of moms and dads advising their children on tricks and techniques for winning, and I didn't want our son to be at a disadvantage.

So I took him out to our backyard to show him some stick horse racing tricks and tips.

The key, I said, was staying focused on running hard no matter what. I demonstrated. Tucking the stick firmly between my legs and running back and forth as fast as I could in our backyard without letting the stick horse slow me down. I did this multiple times before tripping over a small mound of dirt and falling down hard.

As I began to stand back up, I noticed our neighbors, a nice young couple, had come outside to see what was going on and had been watching me run frantically back and forth with a stick horse between my legs.

I limped inside and remembering why I used to make fun of overzealous hyper-competitive parents and vowed never to be one.

Whitewater Rafting with Dad

When I was 13 years old, my parents had recently divorced and my father decided it would be a good time for us to have a father-son bonding weekend.

He planned a trip for us to go whitewater rafting in Snake River Canyon, Wyoming. It was the first and last time I've ever been to Wyoming. Or whitewater rafting, for that matter. But I do have fond and fun memories of what developed into a rather unconventional father-son weekend.

We arrived at Snake River Canyon and were told by the guide that the water was unusually placid and there would be no whitewater rafting, but we could still navigate the river's calm waters, fish, and have cookouts where we stopped to camp. My father, who was once fairly described as having the attention span of a gnat, looked horrified—like it had been announced we'd been kidnapped and wouldn't see civilization again for a very long time.

Although I didn't feel horrified, I suspect I looked seriously concerned. We spent the next eight to 10 hours on a raft. That's it. Just rafting and fishing unsuccessfully. That night we set up camp and had a fire and played backgammon. That's right, backgammon. My father and I played backgammon for a dollar a point. I was down by a lot when we had to quit because the dice rolling kept the others traveling with us awake. Earlier that evening, our tour guide took us inside a cave and pointed out what looked like some Indian drawings. I knew my mom would have found this interesting, but I could tell my dad wasn't even listening and was instead concocting a plan to allow us to escape.

There were some things he knew he couldn't protect me against in the wild. But boredom wasn't one of them. I sensed that a real adventure was about to begin—and not one on the tour guide's itinerary.

The next morning after several more hours on the raft of unsuccessful fishing in calm waters while losing more of my allowance playing backgammon, I realized my father had convinced the tour guide to go a direction that would drop us off at the first small town, which wasn't far away. Suddenly I saw people and a small store. We said goodbye and grabbed the duffel bags I had packed for us.

I had no idea where we were going. My father asked one of the locals for a ride to the nearest airport but he wasn't headed that way. He ended up paying a tall Native American man $50 to allow us to drive his old pickup truck to the nearest airport, where he would pick it up later that day. So there we were: two city boys roughing it but braving the harsh outdoor elements in our own style. The truck had a single 8-track tape: Sgt. Pepper's Lonely Heart Club's Band. I had always liked "Lucy in the Sky with Diamonds," but I got to listen to the entire 8-track during our drive and am too this day a fan of the entire album.

We arrived at a tiny airport with few flights and none that would arrive in destinations more appealing than where we already were, except one -- Las Vegas. As we walked into the hotel lobby in Vegas, we were the only ones checking in with duffel bags. Because I'd only packed outdoor clothing for our rafting trip without Vegas in mind, we bought new clothes more appropriate for the alternate location for our father-son trip. We had room service and I discovered matzo ball soup. This was something that certainly wouldn't have happened had we continued whitewater rafting.

We stayed for a couple of days. I got even playing backgammon with my father and won a little money playing roulette and blackjack (actually, someone played for me while I coached him from the cordoned off area of the casino).

It was a version of father- son bonding, more of a slick citified -- and slightly warped --variety than the rustic rural kind. But it was memorable and had its moments.

We can't cash in casino chips for father's blessings but we can enjoy fun memories and try to find goodness in unexpected places and experiences.

I learned how to improvise, adapt and think out of the box and be open to new experiences. And I am probably the only person out there who hears an invitation to go white water rafting and thinks Sgt. Pepper's Lonely Heart Club's Band, backgammon, Las Vegas, and matzo ball soup and smiles mischievously.

Romantics and Realists

My son Johnny was talking to my wife and me last week and reminded me that I once described myself to him as a "romantic" and my wife, Rebecca, as a "realist" and wanted to know what I meant by that.

I recalled the first experience with Rebecca that made me come to this conclusion and recounted the story best I could.

After my wife and I had been dating for several months we started to discuss the possibility of marriage. We were in our 20's and weren't engaged yet but felt we soon would be and were discussing on a dinner date our love for one another –one of those conversations reminiscent of Billy Joel's song, "I love you just the way you are."

"Would you still love me if I flunked out of law school?" I asked.

"Of course I would," Rebecca reassured me.

But during the course of this otherwise sweet conversation I decided to push the envelope.

"Let's say that instead of going to law school I drove a taxi and never went to college and had no plans of ever going to college, would you still love me and want to marry me?"

Rebecca looked puzzled at me as she thought about my question. "I'm not so sure about that one." She said. "I doubt I would want to marry you if you were that different."

"I would still be me. The same person I am right now. But born into a different economic circumstance and with a different job and background. That's all."

"Yeah, I know. I'm sure you'd be sweet and I would maybe date you but I don't think I would be able to marry you," Rebecca tried to explain. "In my family, college is just very important and I don't think it would occur to me to marry you if you weren't ever going to go to college."

"Really? You wouldn't marry me if I drove a taxi and never planned on going to college?" I responded woundedly. So, I tried to change the hypothetical. "OK. What if I drove a taxi, hadn't gone to college but was considering going to college? Would you marry me then?"

Rebecca said, "That's not a fair question."

"So, you are saying 'no?'" I interjected.

"I guess so," Rebecca said. But added, "It's not fair to ask that and it doesn't make me shallow for saying I wouldn't marry you if you were that different. It's like me asking you if you'd marry me if I was grotesquely overweight right now. I don't think you would."

"That's different." I said. "That's something about you personally that would be different. In my hypothetical, I would be the exact same person I am now– just born into a different environment."

"I don't think there's a difference." Rebecca said.

"Of course there's a difference," I said.

"Well, if there wasn't a difference in our questions, would you marry me if I were really, really overweight?" Rebecca asked again.

"I would marry you for sure if you were 40 pounds overweight," I said. "And it is different."

 "See!" Rebecca exclaimed. "But not if I were 60 pounds overweight?"

"No, I would marry you if you were 60 pounds overweight right now – assuming you wanted eventually get in, you know, better shape for your own health."

"Well, then, if you drove a taxi and hadn't gone to college but eventually wanted to go to college –and maybe even graduate school– I would probably marry you."

"Probably?" I queried.

"OK. I would marry you. But only after you finished college." Rebecca explained.

"Well, I would marry you if you were 60 pounds overweight and wanted eventually to get into better shape – but I wouldn't make you wait until you got in better shape before I would marry you." I said dejectedly. "We're just different, I guess. I must be more of a romantic than you are."

So, that is the difference between a romantic and a realist, in our family anyway. The romantic feels wounded because his hypothetical pronouncements are only 95% reciprocated by the hypotheticals of his realist spouse. And the realist spouse just wants to enjoy eating a nice dinner together while on a date and try to enjoy the moment, which turns out to be more romantic than debating hypotheticals.

The Importance of Ice Cream

Our son moves out tomorrow to go to college. As I drove home late from work my mind was reeling—reeling about the immediate future (getting ready for tomorrow's big event), about the present (the final night at home before our son moves out and moves on) and, of course, about the past (memories which now seem eerily ancient of a boy who is no longer a boy anymore).

My best memory for both my children is what we came to call "ice cream night." For nearly nine years—every Monday night—I would pick up my two kids while my wife had the night to herself. When we started, Johnny was six and Maggie was two. It became a weekly tradition with Dad. We had a routine, and we stuck to it almost without fail. We'd get ice cream --usually at Graeter's -- and then go to Barnes & Noble bookstore for an hour or so, where we'd look at books and magazines, get something to drink like hot chocolate, and make up some activity.

Sometimes we'd play slow motion hide-and-go-seek -- in slow motion so the bookstore employees wouldn't notice what we were doing. Sometimes the kids would make up a play for me in the children's book area. Sometimes I'd read something to one or both of them. Later we'd listen to music or just sit in the cafe and talk. But we were there every Monday night, no matter what. Until one Monday we weren't.

It's hard to persuade a 15-year-old to do much of anything, especially hang out with Dad on Monday nights. But I remember a few years earlier asking my family if they would be on board with me running for Lieutenant Governor. They were. The only hesitation was my son asking if that meant we'd no longer get to do ice cream on Monday nights. I told him softly and candidly, "It might." He looked down at the ground for several seconds but knew something bigger was at stake and then said, "That's OK."

I'll never forget that sweet moment, and I tried to keep our Monday nights going through the campaign. I did a better job than I expected.

Even the state Democratic Party chairman knew Monday nights were a special—even sacred—time for me and my children and would ask frequently during the campaign if I had taken care of business the previous Monday night. I was able to say I had more often than not.

I am grateful for those nine years, now more than ever.

Tonight as I drove home from work I was approaching Graeter's ice cream and decided to call to see if they were still open. They were and so was the Barnes & Noble bookstore across the street. Both stayed open until 10 pm. I called my wife and she got both kids to meet for ice cream again and even joined us herself this time. We were buoyant at the fun irony of it all. We ordered our ice cream and sat and laughed about how we can't go back in time. Perhaps most can't. But tonight I was able to briefly.

I hurried everyone out of Graeter's to go by Barnes & Noble one last time for old time's sake. The kids agreed. We walked through the doors and were greeted by staff offering to help us and reminding us they were going to close in three minutes. I recognized one of them from our earlier days. We all walked up together to the magazine section and lingered for a minute or two, chuckling awkwardly with one another.

And then we were told the store was closing. The kids left and my son drove my daughter home. I stayed inside for a few minutes longer to do a quick once around to see if everything was as I remembered it. It was. And then I unlocked the already locked entrance door and let myself out. And drove home. Alone.

Playing Chess

When my son was four years old, we were up late one night looking for something to do. He grabbed a chess set and asked, "Want to play!?"

Taken aback by his enthusiasm, I said I did but admitted I really didn't know how to play and he'd have to teach me. He said it was easy and to sit down and he'd show me.

I knew Johnny was extremely bright but this was one of those prodigy stories: "Four year old son teaches father how to play chess."

Johnny divided the pieces evenly and set them up for his side and then mine. He then announced, "What we do is slide the pieces across the board and try to knock each other's pieces down. Like in bowling. Whoever knocks down all the pieces first, wins."

"Alright!' I sad. "I think I'm gonna like this chess stuff."

Bon Voyage via Facebook

Dear Rebecca,

Hope the cruise with your friends is going well and you are having fun. I know you said you won't have cell reception but in case any friends with you can see Facebook, I wanted you to know that I did find a can of chili beans for dinner tonight. I mixed in some barbecue sauce and that helped a little.

I also noticed a can a creamed corn in the pantry that you bought several years ago and I can eat that if I'm still hungry later tonight.
Just wanted you to know I'm doing fine and you don't need to worry about me at all.

Sure, I'm a little depressed and lonely but that's my problem and not yours. I just wanted to make sure you aren't thinking about how miserable I am and that you are having a great time on your exciting trip with your really fun friends without me.

Love, John

My Secret Life as a Backgammon Player

Recently, my dear friend, Steve Bass, texted me saying he'd heard I used to be a champion backgammon player and wanted to play me. I loved the idea of being considered a "champion" at anything but mostly was stunned anyone would mention my backgammon past. I hadn't really played in over 35 years and the people I played with back then were in their 40s and 50s –and most of them have died --but I was flattered and couldn't wait to dust off the board and play with my friend.

Backgammon had been my obsession as a teen. I know. right? But let me try to explain. The summer I turned 14, most kids my age were going to camp or playing little league sports or taking on some part-time odd job. The previous summer, I'd worked in the mailroom at my father's company for $1.25 an hour and played little league baseball, though I wasn't much of a baseball player.

But this summer was the first summer after my parent's divorce and I spent it with my father in Ft. Lauderdale, Florida living at a small secluded resort he'd invested in called Le Club International that was famous for its backgammon tournaments.

I'd never heard of backgammon before then. There was a backgammon room attached to the restaurant where people played nightly and a weekly tournament was held. Some of the top backgammon players in the world would visit and play and observers would surround them and watch for hours. I couldn't help but be drawn to the game.

My grandmother Brown had been the first female Life Masters in bridge in Kentucky, so I had a heritage of sorts for cards and board games but none had piqued my interest before backgammon.

I was only 14 and a very sweet little lady in her 50s named Cricket Mathews, who had recently been widowed and who was the National Backgammon Instructor for Le Club, took me under her wing and taught me how to play. Cricket and I would play for hours upon hours, day after day. Initially, she would teach me by commenting on every move I made and telling me what the "right move" was.

I started reading backgammon books and teaching myself too. Soon Cricket wasn't teaching me as much as just playing me, although she never gave up her attitude as my mentor, which I was grateful for. She introduced me to the more serious tournament players and urged me to play in the weekly tournaments, which I did. My first match in a weekly tournament at Le Club was against Arthur Dickman, the top backgammon player in Florida. He made short shrift of me beating me 8-3 but I couldn't wait until the following week to play again. I was hooked.

I never made it to the finals in these weekly tournaments but did get to play against some of the very best backgammon players in the world. When I'd lose to them, I would occasionally ask if they'd give me a lesson or lessons. A few were so surprised and flattered that they agreed. Russ Sands was one and went on to win the World Amateur Backgammon Championship. Baron Vernon Ball, who had just won the World Backgammon Championship, and Lee Genud, who went on to win the Women's World Backgammon Championship and was the top female backgammon player in the world, were two others. (It seems quaint and sexist to even write that women had their own category in some tournaments back then, but they did.)

I returned to Le Club the next summer and visited whenever I could and always spent as much time as possible playing backgammon. I didn't really fit into any of the more traditional groups kids fell into during that period of my life and playing backgammon gave me an identity and something to do that I felt good about. The teen years are a lonely time and backgammon was something I could do alone, if I wanted, playing against myself and studying strategy from the handful of backgammon books available.

Chess was more mainstream but never appealed much to me. Chess is a pure strategy game. Backgammon, which uses dice and has an element of chance, is mostly strategic but also involves a degree of luck. The better player doesn't always win in the short run but inevitably wins over time. I felt life was more like backgammon.

When I came home from my summers in Ft Lauderdale, I wanted to keep playing backgammon, but where? Backgammon had become very popular across the nation during the 1970s and in Louisville there were two clubs, The Prospector and the Louisville Bridge and Backgammon Club.

The Prospector was basically a card and backgammon club in Prospect, Kentucky. Since I wasn't old enough to drive, my mother would drop me off at the Prospector and pick me up (before my bedtime). I'm sure the men there laughed amongst themselves at the curiosity of this scrawny but earnest teen wanting to play backgammon with them. But I loved the rush of walking in and being respected by them because they knew I could beat most of them. They enjoyed humoring me and letting me play against them. Most were very kind and courteous to me. Occasionally, one would get upset at the idea of getting beat by a kid but I learned how to talk to adults and to be both grateful and gracious whether I won or lost.

The summer before I learned how to play backgammon, I had gone to summer camp and received the "Best Sportsmanship Award." My father told me that was the most important award I could have won. I thought he was just trying to make me feel better since it sounded to me like an award given to the person who lost with the best manners, but I think he believed good sportsmanship was important and I did too.

By the time I was 16 and could drive myself, I spent several nights a week at the Louisville Bridge and Backgammon Club in St Mathews. We had weekly tournaments and on non-tournament nights would pair off with someone and play head-to-head for several hours. It wasn't a large group but a sizeable group of interesting characters. Most the regulars were smart, affable and slightly nerdy types. John Shallcross, a recognized local bridge expert, was probably the best backgammon player in the city. Terry Kuchenbrod was an engineer and probably the second best. Terry was a pure mechanic at backgammon and would grind you out over time while John Shallcross was very smart and strategic but also intuitive in a way that couldn't quite be taught and his style of play appealed me. I remember once asking John who he thought would win the Super Bowl that year and he said, "The Philadelphia Eagles seem to be a team of destiny." Terry Kuchenbrod would never have said something like that and instead given a very logical explanation for his answer.

I played in tournaments in Kentucky, Indiana, Georgia and Florida. I never placed but prided myself in being the youngest or second youngest player in these tournaments out of hundreds of participants

The pinnacle of my backgammon career was the Kentucky state tournament in 1980 when I was 17. I was the 6th seed. I don't remember how many total players there were -- and it wasn't a large number -- but it meant a great deal to me that on that afternoon in Frankfort, Kentucky, at the age of 17, my name was written on a chalkboard as the person considered the sixth most likely to win the Kentucky State Backgammon Tournament.

I lost in the second or third round and moved on from backgammon to other interests. When I was 19 and a student at the University of Southern California, I once visited the Cavendish West Club in Los Angeles and played in a backgammon tournament there. In the first round, I played against actor Don Adams, who was Maxwell Smart in the TV series Get Smart. He wasn't thrilled being paired with a teenager but was as polite and as friendly as could be expected. I was fortunate enough to win and wanted to say something clever as I shook his hand like, "Oh and Max, do be careful" but didn't because it didn't seem right. I felt bad beating him. Something about him seemed lonely. I suspect I recognized in him the same loneliness I felt. Backgammon is just a game, after all, and takes up a lot of time that could be used genuinely connecting with other people instead of avoiding doing that while hiding behind playing a board game.

Over this past holiday season we were driving with our children, Johnny and Maggie, to a family dinner and talking about Malcolm Gladwell's book Outliers and whether his 10,000 hour theory was correct (i.e. that if you spend 10,000 hours doing something, especially in your youth, you'll become a true expert at it, like the Beatles playing music or Bill Gates coding software). My children asked me what I did for 10,000 hours in my youth and I answered, "I played backgammon." After a pause, I added "Sorry guys." I explained I should have spent all that time being a better student or becoming really good at something that would have been more beneficial later in life.

But after reflecting more on it, it is a "Sorry, not sorry" sort of thing. Playing backgammon did keep me occupied during my teen years and it developed my mind and gave me a way to fit in, even if it was a somewhat unusual way of fitting in. There was even that time when I was 17 and played in a tournament in Georgia and avoided the consequences back home of being with my best friend who had gotten in a major car accident after a high school party that same weekend.

And there is even a recent example of how backgammon had a positive impact on my life. After my friend and I played backgammon recently, I was on a short vacation with Rebecca and Maggie and they urged me to workout with them in the hotel gym. I went and lifted a few weights but felt out of place and really didn't fit in and was about to leave. Rebecca and Maggie persuaded me to try the treadmill, which I loathe and never stay on longer than a few minutes, but tried anyway. The treadmill had a screen for watching movies or playing a game, including backgammon. I opted for backgammon and set it at the highest level of expertise.

I stayed on the treadmill an average of 40 minutes a day for three days in a row while playing virtual backgammon. On the last day there was a woman on the treadmill next to me running much faster than I was. In fact, I was really only walking fast. I felt embarrassed for myself but I got so engrossed in my backgammon game that I didn't care. Forty minutes later I finished and had beaten the virtual backgammon game at the Mastery Level for the third day in a row and by a large margin each time. I didn't feel so out of place at the hotel gym anymore and even felt a little embarrassed for the virtual backgammon game as I confidently walked out of the gym that day.

A True Fish Tale

I don't have a Bucket List just yet but I do have a "Parent List," a list of about 10 things I want to do with my children before they leave home.

This happened when my son, Johnny, was 10 years old. I had recently checked off "flying kites," and "going fishing" was on deck.

We decided that were doing the a father-son fishing day on a Sunday afternoon and immediately started by packing a picnic basket. True, I had never really been fishing and only imagined what I should do, but a picnic basket seemed like an obvious place to start. My daughter made ham sandwiches and packed them for us.

On the way out the door, I shrewdly remembered we'd be sitting in grass and grabbed a throw blanket for us to sit on while fishing.

We went to Wal-Mart and bought fishing poles. We found a public lake nearby and set up our gear and lay down the throw blanket.

I tried to demonstrate casting for Johnny. "Watch me, honey. This is how you want to do it." I shanked it into the marshy grass.

After untangling it, I realized that, in addition to flubbing the cast, I had not baited the hook. I had forgotten to buy bait and had to improvise.

What to do?

Those ham sandwiches had stringy, soggy slivers of ham that I reasoned could easily be mistaken for a worm by a fish that wasn't paying attention or had below-average fish intelligence.

We baited our lines with slivers of ham and cast them like two men who had never before had to eat what they killed. Our lines intertwined and as we tried to unravel them as it began to rain.

A Fish and Wildlife officer pulled into our lake and walked toward us and as he approached, said, "Good afternoon. Do you gentleman have a fishing license?"

I said, "Oh no, officer! I apologize. I didn't know we needed a fishing license."

The officer looked at the intertwined fishing lines with soggy ham hanging from the hooks and then at the throw blanket we were standing on and said in an almost whisper to me,

"You don't fish much, do you, sir?"

There was really no point in responding. It was what is called a rhetorical question—a device that is rarely used by law enforcement unless the person being questioned has failed so spectacularly at something that further information isn't necessary.

The nice Fish and Wildlife officer let us off with a warning and we packed our belongings and sat in the car waiting for the rain to let up, splitting the second ham sandwich. My son noted, "I've never been arrested before, Dad."

I explained this whole episode would help with his "street cred" at school but that he should not give too much detail about the cause of our brush with the law. We both seemed to like the idea of feeling a little like outlaws, especially if it meant not having to fish.

Afterwards we drove to a more modern place for fathers and sons— where we played video games and miniature golf and raced go-karts.

None of which were on my "Parent List," which I have since thrown away.

Honoring My Son's Choices

My wife and I heard about other parents putting monitoring software on their children's laptops and we decided to join in and began monitoring our 12 year old son's internet activity. As I looked over the first week's batch of websites, I was pleased to see there were no "inappropriate" websites visited.

Just a lot of gaming websites and an unusually high number of political websites visited. However, upon closer examination, I noticed almost all the political websites were republican-leaning.

I didn't know what to do. I was a Democrat and so was most everyone in my family.

Was my son a closet Republican?

Was this the kind of thing I should talk to my child about alone or should I involve a counselor?

Was seven conservative-leaning websites visited coupled with a Google search for Glenn Beck in a two-week period grounds for an intervention?

Or should I take a more compassionate approach and explain that some of my closest friends are republican and that this is nothing to be ashamed of?

I could even recommend online groups and organizations for people who eventually make conservatism a "life choice."

As my head was spinning with what to do, I heard a loud and deeply aggravated voice from upstairs yell "Daaaaad!"— and yelled in that way that I knew I was in trouble. My 12 year old son marched down the stairs and announced he had discovered the spy software and wanted it removed immediately.

I explained I was leaving it on for his own benefit and because it was my duty as a parent.

He then declared that I was violating his First Amendment rights and demanded I remove the spyware.

I was not expecting a constitutional argument. I was surprised and impressed. I started to explain how the Constitution didn't apply in this circumstance, but I was so proud of his passion and bold effort, I asked for his laptop and removed the spyware.

That was six years ago. Some nights when Johnny's out driving and it's late, I worry. I question my decision and think to myself, "I hope Johnny is safe and hasn't gotten sucked in to hanging out with a group of young Republicans staying up late talking about Ronald Reagan or supply-side economics.

Then I remind myself as a parent, I can only do so much and when I was his age, my parents worried about much worse with me. I take comfort knowing whatever Johnny is doing, he can make a compelling argument that it is protected under the US Constitution.

Halloween Heroism

When my son Johnny was four years old, he dressed up like Batman. He was dressed in full character and kept the mask on at all times. Although only four, Johnny was a very friendly and talkative child.

We stopped by Blockbuster before Trick-or-Treating to rent a movie and there were two Goth-looking teenagers, too cool for Halloween, who glanced at us and gave us a dismissive look—as if to say "A father and son on Halloween. How lame."

They had piercings all over, tattoos and Goth attire. Even though I was in my mid 30s, rebellious teens intimidated me so I nudged Johnny and moved away from them.

When I wasn't looking, Johnny had slipped away from me. I heard Johnny's voice and he was making conversation with the two teens.

I walked toward them worried he was going to get his feelings hurt.

"Hey you guys!" I heard Johnny say cheerfully to them. "I'm Batman." He got no response. Just a look of jaded disgust from the teens.

Then Johnny added, "So who are you guys dressed up as?"

It was a total smack down of the two teens by a 4-year-old. I stopped and watched and tried to contain my laughter. They were speechless and humiliated as they sighed and slinked out of the door.

Johnny didn't understand what had happened but I was proud Batman had my back that night and I had a new Halloween hero.

Chick-fil-A's Market Strategy

It used to be, if you were hungry for chicken and in a hurry—and against gay marriage—there wasn't a clear fast food option.

Not anymore.

Chick-fil-A has finally articulated what most suspected. They want to dominate the market share of the heterosexual, chicken-eating population by coming out against gay marriage.

No surprises here. I mean, c'mon. "Chick" is in the name.

I'll be watching next month for the new Chick-fil-A "Hetero Combo," featuring a masculine-looking sandwich with two chicken breasts and straight-looking garnishes.

This creates a frenzy among the remaining fast food chicken chains to see who will try to appeal to the gay-friendly, chicken-eating population.

Apparently rumors that Popeye's is considering moving their headquarters to Fire Island, New York, and that KFC is introducing the "Judy Garland Over the Rainbow" sandwich are false. However, it does appear that Dairy Queen is working on playing both sides with the "Big Butch Chicken Basket"

Gallbladder-less

Outsourcing and downsizing have impacted every segment of our economy. Our bodies are no different.

Today, after over five decades together, I am parting ways with my gallbladder.

I would like to thank my gallbladder for 55 years of a very successful partnership and reliable digestion, even during times when my diet was almost exclusively fatty and spicy foods.

Although there was disagreement about the need for gallstones, this was a mutually agreed on decision that in no way reflects poorly on my gallbladder. We both felt it was time to explore other opportunities.

All former gallbladder roles will be taken over by my liver which welcomes the new challenge and feels more ready than ever to successfully take on these additional obligations.

My digestive system looks forward to a more efficient future and is confident it will be able to do more with less.

Matters of the Heart

I was doing a follow-up appointment with my primary care physician after my recent gall bladder surgery and he pointed out that one of the attending physicians reviewing the scan of my midsection saw calcium deposits in my heart area and concluded on my report that I had CAD (coronary artery disease). Not an acronym I ever wanted to see under my name but there it was.

It was merely a footnote on my report but because of my family history with heart disease, my doctor wanted me to do some additional tests with a cardiologist and recommended a CT scan and an echo stress test

I consider myself at that age in life where I no longer go to the doctor expecting good news like "Well, everything looks great!" That period ended in my mid-40s. Nowadays, it's "Well, there's good news and bad news" which really means there's just bad news because the good news is that the bad news isn't as bad as it could be.

A few years ago my doctor told me I had a particular condition but that "I would probably die of something else" and to "try not to worry about it." I asked him if he would worry about it if he were in my shoes and he said, "I'm not the best person to ask because I tend to worry a lot and probably would." We both laughed but he laughed harder.

This is life at 55. You may not have a literal limp just yet but you probably have collected enough health issues to at least feel you have a figurative limp. It's a slow erosion of the spirit that vanquishes that former sense of invincibility enjoyed in youth that now is difficult even to recall.

The nurses who check your vitals and tell you there's no need to take your shirt off, merely underline the indignity of moving into this new category of patient which requires focused attention to avoid overlooking the next level of deterioration.

As my doctor looked over all my old heart-related tests, he asked if I ever had chest pains or shortness of breath after walking up several flights of stairs. I told him "no" to the first question and "possibly" to the second one but that I wasn't sure.

The next morning I had a business meeting and decided to walk up a single flight of stairs instead of taking the elevator to see how I'd do. I did have very slight shortness of breath but as I sat in the meeting wondering how serious it was, my anxiety grew and I started to mildly hyperventilate and for the next 40 minutes struggled to breathe normally, not because of actual plaque build-up in my heart but because of worrying about possible plaque build-up. I joked with someone about it after the meeting and was fine after that but I took the elevator to the lobby when leaving to be safe.

My CT Scan was scheduled a few days later and took only a few minutes lying on a large table while a scan was done of my torso. I started to take my shirt off before getting on the table, but the male nurse said that wouldn't be necessary and attached some wires to my chest and a few moments later I was finished.

When I got my CT scan results I was told I'd moved from "mild" to "moderate" risk for a heart attack and that the echo stress test a few days later would determine if the plaque was currently causing any problems. It was suggested I start taking a baby aspirin daily and to eat more fruits and vegetables and exercise 40 minutes 4 times a week. And, as a precautionary measure, I was prescribed nitroglycerin "just to have on hand" in the unlikely event I ever experienced angina.

As I walked out of the hospital, I felt my figurative limp turning into a literal one. Or at least developing into a stoop.

I called Rebecca and told her the results. "This is good that you are getting on top of this early," she told me. "I think this is good news." I countered that it didn't feel like good news at all to me. I pointed out that I had just been told I had a 15% chance of having a heart attack. I left out that it was a 15% chance over a 10 year period but I was trying to make a point. Rebecca was unfazed and told me again she was encouraged that I was being proactive.

When I got home Rebecca was sitting on the bed talking to a friend on the phone. I puttered around the bathroom waiting for her conversation to end but she continued talking. I stepped into the bedroom and showed Rebecca my nitroglycerin glycerin bottle and she nodded and waved that she understood what it was and kept talking to her friend. A few minutes later I opened the drawer in the bathroom that Rebecca could see from where she was sitting and pointed to where I was going to put the nitroglycerin bottle in case we ever needed it. Rebecca smiled and waved giving me a thumbs-up. After a few more minutes, I pointed underneath my tongue and whispered, "The nitroglycerin pill goes right here just under the tongue if I ever need one." Rebecca waved pleasantly again and motioned that she understood as she chatted away with her friend.

As much as I wanted sympathy, it wasn't going to happen.

A few days later it was time for my echo stress test -- the test that would let me know if all this added up to genuine bad news or good news meaning that things aren't as bad as they could be.

My cardiologist is truly wonderful and I can't imagine a more caring or thorough cardiologist anywhere. We looked over the ECG and it looked surprisingly good. Next, it was time for the dreaded treadmill test. He told me that he wanted me to go as long as I possibly could, "until I was ready to collapse," and I promised I would.

"Most guys your age do about 9 minutes."

That's all I needed to hear. I wasn't leaving the treadmill until I'd been on for well over 9 minutes.

All was going well at 4 minutes which was the first checkpoint. The next checkpoint was 8 minutes and I was still going strong. The doctor checked back again at 9 minutes and told me I was doing well and keep going as long as I possibly could. At 12 minutes it was getting painful and I was clearly winded but undeterred. I closed my eyes and kept going. At 13 minutes my doctor was clearly impressed and told me, "If you're too tired, it's OK to stop now." A few seconds later he added, "It's up to you, John, but we have all the information we need so you can stop if you want." I motioned to stop the treadmill and exhaustedly fell on the table to catch my breath.

My doctor told me I went 13 minutes and 36 seconds, which was great, but then added that he had done 14 minutes on his last stress test.

I didn't say anything but wondered if he urged me to stop early so I wouldn't beat his time.

"How are you feeling?" he asked.

"Good." I paused. "I may have been able to make it to 14 minutes if I'd really pushed myself." I couldn't resist.

"Maybe next time," he responded. "I hope you do eventually catch me" before adding "Of course, I'm 7 years older than you are."

OK. That was it. Game on!

He told me my heart function looked very good and to make the diet and exercise changes he suggested and that we'd do another stress test in 3 years. Nothing more was needed at this time. It was nice getting good news for a change.

Will I beat 14 minutes on my stress test 3 years from now? Of course, I will. It's all but guaranteed. Sure I may be anxious and needy but I'm also extremely competitive and now I have the motivation that's been missing.

They say the quickest way to a man's heart is through his stomach. Maybe so. But the quickest way to motivate some men to protect their heart health may be to get their competitive dander up.

The fact they ask you to take your shirt off to wire you up for the treadmill test only helps.

My heart now appears to have a hopeful future.

Comparing Ourselves

You know the people I'm talking about. The ones that make you think about where you are in life and wonder if you are good enough..

Just now I am parked in Staples' parking lot waiting for the store to open. I'm in my maroon Honda Accord, an empty sack of Chick-fil-A on the passenger floorboard. I am 50 years old wearing khaki pants and a button down striped shirt and wavy disheveled hair.

While waiting, I have my laptop open and am posting on Facebook about my dog going to the bathroom in my office this morning.

Then a shiny jet black regal looking car drives up beside me. It is a BMW and seems to clear it's throat so I will notice. The driver is also about 50 and is wearing a dark pin striped suit and a heavily starched white dress shirt with a striped tie with a tie clip. His hair is combed back immaculately in perfect rows standing at attention proudly with just the right amount of product. Thin frame bifocals and a serious stern look as he looks straight ahead waiting for Staples to open.

I hope he looks over at me and reflects for a few moments and asks himself, "How did I ever become such a boring loser?"

I doubt he even has a Facebook account.

Children are God's way of Keeping Adults Humble.

I recently attended a Father-Daughter weekend at my daughter's college and my son came with me.

The first night I met a lot of the fathers and the next day while having lunch with my children I asked, "Who was the short chubby dad sitting at our table?"

Without a moment's hesitation both my kids answered simultaneously: "Um, that was you, Dad."

First Sunday as Empty Nesters

After church, Rebecca drops me off at home and leaves to celebrate an aunt's birthday.

I go to our bedroom and lie on the bed and wait for Rebecca to get back. At 2pm I text Rebecca asking what time she'll be back. She says around 3:30 or 4pm.

I don't turn on the TV but get out my laptop and pass the time looking at pictures of "35 celebrities who haven't aged well." I look at all 35 celebrities. Spoiler alert: Val Kilmer has not aged well at all.

It's now 3pm and I text Rebecca again and she says she's on her way home. I doze off and am awakened as she walks in. I get up and putter around the bedroom to make it look like I've been busy doing something.

I mumble, "I'm glad you're back."

Rebecca, somewhat surprised, smiles and asks, "Did you miss me?" I smile sheepishly, "I did miss you."

"I missed you, too," Rebecca answers. This empty nest thing is going to be OK.

How to Survive a Winter Storm and Find Your Inner Hero

As we hunker down tonight for Kentucky's Blizzard-Palooza, I am reminded of an even bigger storm I endured over 20 years ago and, as awful as it was, I remember in an oddly endearing way.

I was a newlywed and recent law school graduate and had just moved to Tamarac, Florida, to start a new job in Ft. Lauderdale. I chose Tamarac because I was able to get a great deal on a condo rental and had rented it sight unseen.

As we drove into Tamarac, we noticed it wasn't the young hip town we had hoped it would be. Instead, it was a retirement community. The first restaurants we saw were all buffet restaurants and each block seemed dotted with prosthetic stores. I admitted to Rebecca I probably should have researched Tamarac better but encouraged her to look on the bright side: it was a great deal, we wouldn't have rowdy neighbors, and hey, it was Florida.

We found our pink pastel retirement condo, unpacked, rented some movies at Blockbuster, and got dressed up and headed out for our first big date night in Florida.

We got home late and Rebecca flipped on the television and yelled for me to come quickly.

"What is it?" I asked.

Rebecca pointed to the TV, "Look! They are warning that a major hurricane is coming tomorrow and saying we should evacuate immediately."

"Nah," I muttered reassuringly. "It's Florida. They have hurricanes all the time. We'll be fine."

We turned off the TV went to bed and didn't wake up until noon the next day.

105

We leisurely headed to the grocery to stock our new home but noticed the grocery was busy—crazily busy—and many of the shelves had been cleared.

We bought a few items and headed home to find out more about this hurricane. It was Hurricane Andrew.

I still wasn't overly concerned. I'd been through hurricanes before. But Rebecca hadn't and was getting worried.

I decided to try to be the strong protective husband I sensed my wife and our small shih tzu, Julep, were yearning for me to be. Since the grocery stores had limited choices, I went to Miami Subs and bought a half dozen submarine sandwiches. I proudly showed Rebecca how I'd outsmarted our bleak circumstances and made sure we wouldn't be without food.

But instead of being relieved, Rebecca looked more nervous than before and told me she thought we should evacuate like everyone else. She had been watching the news and miles of streaming cars were leaving south Florida in a mass exodus.

"Look," I implored. "How many times will we get to say we lived through one of the worst storms in modern U.S. history?" I paused. "Think about it." I paused again. "This is historic."

As I jabbered on, I noticed fearful tears welling up in Rebecca's eyes. "What about Julep?" She asked. "What if we all die?"

I felt a lump welling in my throat and despite my brilliant sub sandwich maneuver, I was beginning to second-guess the wisdom of my plan to stare down Hurricane Andrew.

We looked again at the TV and now it was eerily quiet outside—the chilling calm before the storm.

Reporters were telling us the roads were now clear; the city had been evacuated and those who stayed behind were hunkering down to brave the storm.

"Get the dog," I said resignedly. "We're leaving."

Rebecca hugged me, got Julep and a change of clothes, and we hopped in the car and were off.

We had a clear shot all the way to north Florida as we outran Hurricane Andrew. It was a bizarre consolation prize for my foolhardy delay.

We were nearing the Georgia border and now were exhausted and ready to find a hotel room for the night. But tens of thousands of others had the exact same thought and started hours before us. Hotel after hotel told us they were full. At about 5 am we were nearing Valdosta, GA and found a La Quinta Inn. There was a single room available someone had reserved but they hadn't shown up, and the manager graciously gave it to us. We didn't dare tell the manager about Julep in case they had a "no pet" policy. I tucked Julep under my arm and smuggled her by the manager and she thankfully didn't yelp.

The next day we took it easy and reflected on how grateful we were that we fled and were safe and dry in a nice hotel with electricity. We stayed a second night and the next morning I called the University of Kentucky law school to see if final grades had been posted. I called from the phone in the hotel room and gave the administrator my social security number while still on my knees, where I had just prayed fervently for good grades so I could graduate.

"Yes! Yes! Yes! Yes!" I yelled into a pillow to muffle the sound of my ecstatic scream when I received the merciful news I had graduated from law school.

We decided it was time to head home to survey the damage and face the consequences. We pulled in just before nightfall and to our amazement our condo building hadn't been hit at all. We even had electricity. We had remarkably been spared.

Other towns nearby, like Kendall and Homestead, were nearly decimated: 25,000 homes were destroyed and 100,000 more damaged. Over a million homes were without electricity—many for weeks.

Twenty-six people died, and property damage totaled over $26 billion. Hurricane Andrew was the most destructive hurricane in American history.

We went inside and threw away the four extra sub sandwiches, unpacked, and turned on the TV just as if nothing had happened since we turned it off two days earlier.

It's truly amazing how quickly we can return to normalcy after just being spared major devastation.

A few days later I returned the movies we had rented from Blockbuster and was charged a late fee. I argued that Blockbuster should waive the late fee because the hurricane was an "act of God" that caused me to flee the city for several days and return the movies late. I tried explaining in a lawyerly fashion that these clauses were in all contracts and called a force majeure clause. The teenaged clerk looked at me like I was a jerk, which I was. But that didn't stop me.

"Look, I'm a lawyer," I explained. "Trust me. This is not something you want to fight me on."

The clerk told me he'd have to talk to his manager the next day but had to charge me the late fee for now. I shrugged and paid the late fee and strutted out of Blockbuster as dauntingly as I could in a T-shirt.

I probably hadn't impressed my teen accuser, but I told myself I had grown a lot the week of the storm. I was now a law school graduate and just had my first legal run-in over a movie rental late charge and, despite losing, had made some forceful legal points.

And, of course, I now was a survivor of a major storm.

I got into my car and headed back to my pink pastel condo where I was sure my wife and shih tzu were waiting eagerly for their hero to return home.

Somewhere tonight in Kentucky there are some newly married young couples awaiting the avalanche of snow and fearful they won't know how to handle it. Fear not. This may be the night you find your hero's voice. Or maybe it won't be and you'll end up like me with only a memorable story about how you survived Kentucky's winter storm in 2016. Either is fine as long as you are lucky enough to come out unscathed.

My advice? Do what they say on the news and don't buy into any plans involving submarine sandwiches.

Is Chivalry Dead?

Some claim chivalry is dead. But not in Louisville, Kentucky.

As I was leaving an event the other night, I walked outside with a group of people including my friend, Tammy York-Day. I decided to walk Tammy to the multilevel parking lot nearby where we both had parked as any Southern gentleman would be expected to do.

It was dark out and as we peered into the parking garage it was eerily quiet.

I had parked on the second floor and Tammy had parked on the fourth floor.

"What does modern day chivalry command?" I wondered to myself.

OK. I didn't really wonder that to myself. What I really thought to myself was Oh, no! Am I expected to go all the way up to the fourth floor with Tammy and pretend like I am going to protect her? I didn't say this out loud. I just thought it.

And then thought, "I really don't want to do that. It's two extra full floors up and it is late and, frankly, I'm a little scared to go up there with only Tammy to protect me." I didn't say that out loud either.

My mind immediately went into overdrive to quickly come up with an alternative plan. One that was still within the realm of chivalry but not overly or absurdly chivalrous.

Instead of walking toward the elevator, I started up the stairs. I let Tammy take the elevator. It would be harder, I reasoned, for Tammy to expect me to walk up two extra flights of stairs than I needed to for my car. And I figured since her car was on the fourth floor, Tammy would prefer the elevator and she did.

But my real save was I yelled out to Tammy as I said good-bye, "I promise to wait here on the stairs until you get to your car and I will listen for sounds of scuffling or screaming. If you get mugged or attacked just scream as loudly as you can."

I continued explaining my chivalrous plan: "I will be able to hear you because a scream from the fourth floor of the parking garage will carry to the second floor, where I will be with my car. Then I will start screaming and from the second floor, my scream would be heard at the street level, and hopefully someone would hear me and come to your rescue."
Someone other than me, that is.

It was a brilliant, fool-proof, and yet still chivalrous plan.

But as we stood at the stairs and elevator, it became obvious to me Tammy was wondering what would happen if she was attacked then and there. I knew exactly how to calm her worries. I reassured Tammy that even though I wasn't a tall or strong guy, I did have a big vocabulary and could use sarcasm—biting sarcasm, if necessary --that would knock back any attacker who was foolish enough to try to harm her.

Although she didn't say anything, I imagined Tammy felt safe and secure with a Southern gentleman standing in the stairwell a dozen feet away waiting for her to take the elevator.

As I waved goodbye and promised to wait to see if she screamed from the fourth floor, Tammy must have known one thing for sure: chivalry was far from dead tonight in Louisville, Kentucky.

Big Shot on a Budget

Every month I have dinner with a wonderful group of guys we call The Club. It's a fun collection of lawyers, judges, businessmen and politicos. Typically, we each pay for our own dinner, but every few months someone felt the need to be a bigshot and would pick up the check for the group. After several years of The Club dinners, I had never picked up the tab felt it may be my time. Tonight I announced I would "probably" be covering for all of us and, admittedly, did enjoy sounding like a bigshot – at least a tentative bigshot.

As we were finishing dinner, I furtively slipped by the cashier and asked how much our table's dinner would be because I might be picking up the check. The cashier pointed to a much higher figure than I had imagined and explained that a 15% gratuity was automatically added since there were more than seven of us. I told her I would not be picking up the check this time after all but maybe I could buy dessert for the table.

The dessert menu reached the table and no one ordered anything. Hmmmm. Now what?

I suddenly had creative solution that just might work!

I went back to the cashier and said, "Look, how 'bout I pay for 25% of the bill? Can you work that out for me?"

The cashier politely said it shouldn't be a problem but added that no one had ever made that request before.

"How would that work?" she asked.

"Well," I said, "Just take 25% off the top and charge everyone else only 75% of their meal."

I looked at her incredulously like this was a routine request in large groups where the big shot is also fiscally prudent.

A few minutes later she came by and whispered in my ear, "Does that

25% off the top include the tip?"

"Yes," I said. "Look, just charge me one-quarter of the total price and divide up the remainder evenly—including the tip."

At this point the person next to me – a true bigshot-- said, "Just give me the check. I'll cover it."

I insisted on paying 25%, and a small verbal scuffle over the bill ensued.

"Oh, are you serious about getting 25% of the tab? I thought you were joking," said the true bigshot.

"I'm completely serious!" I exclaimed, hoping someone else at the table would notice. "Why don't you pick up the remaining 75%?" And he did.

I announced to the table that although I wasn't picking up the entire tab, I was covering 25%.

I added I would be picking up 25% of a meal this summer and another 25% of a meal in the fall and then again next spring so that I would incrementally pick up 100% of one of our group dinners. It was just going to stretch out over an 18 month period.

As we shook hands and said goodbye until next month's dinner, I tried to simplify things for how to thank me and my true bigshot friend for tonight's dinner.

'You know those au gratin potatoes you had tonight? Well, I paid for them. Someone else picked up the entree, drink, and salad. So just thank me for the au gratin potatoes."

As brilliant as my plan seemed initially, I ended up spending more than I had planned to feel like a bigshot and looked cheaper than ever.

Turns out that showing off, like fine dining menus, is hard to pull off a la carte.

Christmas Preparations

A few Christmases ago when our children were still Santa age – and before Christmas became more of a business transaction -- my job was to work the wee hours of the morning assembling a miniature pool table in our basement and surprise our children Christmas morning.

I started around 1 am. By 3 am I was almost finished but realized I had assembled one of the short ends of the table upside down. So, I took the entire thing apart and started over.

By 4:30 am I was nearly finished again before realizing I had inadvertently assembled one of the long ends of the table upside down. I took a short break to say as many curse words as I could recall at that time of morning and got back to work just before 5 am.

I took apart the table again and decided to get out the directions this time. I didn't make any mistakes this last time but did run out of time because, frankly, I'm just not good at putting things together.

It was now 6:30 am and I heard feet pattering upstairs and cries of "Dad, where are you?"

Johnny and Maggie were ready to see what Santa had left them and weren't going to give me another half hour to finish Santa's work for him. Fortunately, I was quick on my feet with a solution.

A personal note from Santa explaining what happened.

> *Dear Johnny and Maggie, Merry Christmas!!*
>
> *I love you both very much and hope you like all the presents I left you, including the miniature pool table.*
>
> *As you know, I have to cover a lot of ground tonight and in my old age don't move as quickly as I used to. I almost got the pool table set up, but had to leave before finishing to get to all the other children in the world. I left the last few pieces for your father to finish putting together for you.*

Thanks for the cookies and milk.

Merry Christmas!!! S.C.

Johnny and Maggie were excited about the miniature pool table but disappointed Santa had left it up to me to finish putting together because they knew how lousy I was at that sort of thing.

I think this was the Christmas that Santa began to lose his credibility.

How Bookstores Can Save the World

Yesterday, I was in Barnes & Noble bookstore and browsed three different sections.

Politics section. It seemed like every book title was about blaming somebody or some group or something for all of our problems.

Self-help section. All the titles in this section seemed to be about taking responsibility for yourself and not blaming others and making the most of your life.

Humor section. The books in this section had fun and frivolous titles that make a mockery of our day-to-day world and help lighten our load and restore our perspective.

So here's my big idea to save the world:

Take the self-help books and place them in the Politics section. That way we will help end the blame game and start thinking about what we each can do to make things better.

Take all the books in the Humor section and place them in the Self-Help section. Frankly, having a good laugh or two each day is better than buying and reading an entire new book we won't act on anyway.

And, finally, place all the books from the Politics section in the Humor section. Those books will then be properly categorized and are a lot funnier than most the books in that section anyway, if you actually try to take them seriously. And they will stop being confused for books that teach or inform and finally serve a useful purpose.

The Professor Who Changed My Life

At the age of 54, I finally finished something I started 35 years ago: a second bachelor's degree in philosophy.

My first B.A was in history three decades ago but when I graduated I was just 6 hours shy of a second degree in my original major, philosophy. I always wanted to eventually complete that second degree and I'm glad I did. Not so much because I have a deep personal commitment to the study of philosophy but because of the personal significance of how I came to declare philosophy as my original major.

In 1982 I was a freshman in college at the University of Southern California. I was on probation as a transfer student and struggling to survive in my new academic environment. I had been a lazy and mediocre student in high school and appeared to lack the discipline and maturity necessary to succeed in college. I had gotten way behind in my philosophy course, Reasoning and Critical Thinking, and decided I would drop the course in the next day or two.

I was sitting alone in my room combing through a medical reference book I kept handy. I was a hypochondriac and coped with my generalized anxiety by diagnosing myself with various medical conditions and diseases. Of course, I never really had any of these ailments but seemed to get some sort of perverse enjoyment out of worrying that I might.

This particular day I had decided I had a dire kidney disorder when my phone rang.

There was no caller ID in 1982, so I answered. "Hello, is this John?"

"Yes," I answered. "Who is this?"

"This is Morris Engel, your philosophy professor, and I noticed you haven't been to class for several weeks."

"Uh, um. Hi, Professor Engel. I apologize for my absences. I think I may have something called acute renal failure and will probably have to drop your class."

"I'm very sorry to hear about your medical situation, John." Professor Engel responded. "Why don't you come in and see me tomorrow and I'll help you get caught up so you don't have to drop."

I was so stunned by the call and the offer that I didn't know what else to say except, "OK."

The next day I met Professor Engel in his office and he patiently walked me through the first few weeks' assignments and told me that if I wouldn't drop, he'd allow me to take just half the test with the rest of the class the next day and the second half during class two days later.

I was so touched with the personal attention he was giving me that I agreed and studied harder than I ever had and completed the tests.

The following class the student next to me said, "So, are you the famous Mr. Brown?" I smiled awkwardly as she explained Professor Engel (while I was taking the second half of the test) scolded the rest of the class for doing so poorly and pointed out a student named Mr. Brown, who was about to drop the course, had gotten a 100% and the only A on the first half of the exam.

I couldn't believe it.

It was the first time in years I had gotten attention for doing well in school. I sat through the remainder of that class a slightly different -- and more confident-- person. Maybe I did have what it takes to succeed in college.

I continued to want to please Professor Engel and worked harder than I ever had as a student. Professor Engel wrote both books used in his class. That impressed me. I'd never been around scholarly people before and really admired him.

A few weeks later, after doing well on the second exam, Professor Engel suggested I consider majoring in philosophy and even invited me to attend a philosophy conference in Northern California. I didn't attend the conference but did declare a major in philosophy.

I made an "A" in the course, my first "A" in college. I signed up and took a second philosophy course the next term with Professor Engel and made my second college "A." I had gone from being a flailing student on the verge of dropping out of college to a serious, hard-working and very motivated student ---thanks to a single professor who believed in me.

I eventually did move home and transferred to Bellarmine University and changed my major to history. I joked that I decided to major in philosophy because, as Socrates said, the unexamined life isn't worth living but switched to history because I decided the over-examined life wasn't worth living either. But I kept a soft spot in my academic heart for philosophy. Before graduating from college, I made over 30 more A's and graduated with high honors. I then went on to law school and later completed an MBA at age 40. I even taught college part-time myself as an adjunct professor for several years.

I can't emphasize enough the importance in my life that the phone call from Professor S Morris Engel had on me 35 years ago. His reaching out to me, taking the time to help, and then telling me in various ways he believed in me is the very essence of what it means to be a great teacher. And it changed the course of my life for the better.

If you are a teacher and happen to be reading this, know how important you are and can be every day. You have the power to dramatically change the direction of a young person's life in important and positive ways.

I never got to thank Professor Engel for what he did for me but for

$9.95 it's amazing the information you can find on the internet. He is still alive and I just found his phone number. If his call to me changed my life, the least I can do is call and thank him and I plan to do just that.

I'm excited to talk to Professor Engel, who retired a few years ago and is now in his mid 80's. He taught his entire adult life and authored a dozen books on philosophy.

I can't wait to tell him that I finally finished my commitment to earn a philosophy degree — some 35 years later — and to thank him for having such a profound influence on my life. For teaching me how to think and to love the pursuit of wisdom.

I can also let him know that I fortunately survived my imaginary battle with acute renal failure and hopefully we can both laugh at the lame excuses students concoct as they wait to find someone who believes in them.

After multiple failed attempts to reach Professor Engel, I finally heard from his two sons that he did receive my letter on the weekend of Father's Day. He read it several times and was deeply touched.

I teared up myself with joy and gratitude that I finally got to properly thank a teacher who changed my life.

Remembering Maddie

I didn't know Maddie Yates or her family but my heart goes out to them tonight.

Maddie is the Louisville high school student who committed suicide yesterday after posting a video explaining her plan to kill herself and why.

The video is no longer on the internet but the transcript is. I just read the transcript and was drawn to this part:

"Remember how bad of a person I really am. I say awful things. Even if I don't mean them, I say them. You don't even want to know the things that I think; I am not a good person. I'm doing literally the whole world a favor."

I was drawn to these words because I wish more adults would say from time to time –and say it so a young person can hear it:

"I say awful things that I don't mean and later regret saying. I think thoughts that no good person would think. I sometimes wonder to myself how someone like me could ever be a 'good person.' But that doesn't make me a bad person. It makes me about average–and the same can be said for everyone else who has thoughts like this. We just aren't very good at talking openly about the uncomfortable parts of ourselves… but maybe one day we'll get better at it."

And I think if each of us adults would say something like that from time to time –and say it so a young person can hear it–I think we would be doing literally the whole world a favor.

Flight Attendant Revenge

I am on a flight right now and not speaking to my flight attendant. She asked me twice to turn off my mobile device and then checked to make sure I hadn't turned it back on as she walked past me a third time before takeoff. And she said it to me in a really stern and authoritative way that made me feel like I was talking in class in 2nd grade, like the time Ms.

White at Wilder Elementary pulled me several feet out of my chair by my hair—in front of the whole class.

She doesn't know I'm not speaking to her. She thinks I didn't even notice her sassiness and that I was glad to have her remind me to turn off my cell phone before we start taxiing.

I would never want to do anything to endanger any flight I am on. I have volunteered many times to sit by the exit door in case of an emergency. She probably doesn't even know that.

To get even with her, I am squinting my eyes at her while she isn't looking. And thinking of the term "stewardess" instead of "flight attendant." But I know that is probably hitting below the belt, even though I am only saying it in my mind.

Oh, brother! Now the guy two seats in front of me—who turned off his mobile device after she asked the first time—is joking around with the flight attendant and she is being all chummy with him. Teacher's pet! And it is no accident he is just two seats away from me. She is trying to rub it in.

Here she comes with the beverage cart. I just shook my head when she asked if I wanted a beverage. Even though I am thirsty. I didn't speak a single word. Silent treatment. I even let her look at my computer screen while I wrote this post. The font was too small to read, but I think she knew she had crossed a line earlier with me by the way I gave such a pouty, wounded, non-verbal "no thanks" to her free beverage offer.

And just because I am posting this on Facebook doesn't make me petty. Seriously. I was already petty long before this. I just hope we both learned a useful lesson from this experience. Actually, I really hope only she did.

I'll put it this way: she's just lucky they aren't serving lunch on this flight for me to politely and non-verbally decline. Even though I am really hungry.

Looking Into Your Future

During a recent service at church, my wife and I sat behind a couple about 25 years older than us and I kept staring at them. I wondered if that's what Rebecca and I would look like in 25 years. I figured getting dressed up and going to church was probably the highlight of their week. I can't imagine they do much else that is all that fun. They didn't seem to have great chemistry and, frankly, had not aged all that well. I'm sure they are very nice people but it left me a little sad and concerned.

A few minutes into the sermon they both got up and left. I figured it was incontinence.

As they walked past me I smiled and nodded to them and then looked behind me and noticed a chipper young couple about 25 years younger than Rebecca and me sitting right behind us. And they were looking at me. Both of them. And they weren't smiling.

I wanted to turn around and tell them, "Look, I still got it going on. I really do."

But that would have been wildly inappropriate. So I just sat there and made sure I didn't leave early and raise any questions about my continence.

It's your loss, Honey.

My wife is working on something in our bedroom and asked me if I had time to help by doing her a favor..... I explained that I had a pile of busywork to finish and couldn't help right now. Rebecca understood and I went back to my office in our home.

But before getting down to work, I saw I had left a basketball in the office from earlier. Feeling fidgety, I picked up the ball and tried to spin it on my finger, like I used to as a boy. I was a little rusty at first... but by the third try it was the ball spinning equivalent of riding a bicycle. You don't forget how to do it.

This was exciting to me.

So I took the ball and walked into our bedroom where Rebecca was working away and I started tossing the ball up and down while pacing casually and trying to think of how to bring up the topic most naturally, of seeing if she'd like to see me spin the basketball on my finger.

But before I could ask anything, Rebecca looked up at me and said, "What are you doing in here? I am busy now and I thought you told me you had work to do."

"I do." I said. "Have work to do." I paused and acted like I had been working and was confused how I ended up back in our bedroom holding a basketball. I looked at her and thought one last time about asking her if she wanted to see me spin the basketball on my finger.

"What do you want?" Rebecca asked. "Seriously? Are you just going to stand there? I really have a lot to do now."

I just shrugged and said, "I have a lot to do too." And mumbled under my breath "Probably even more than you" as I slinked out of the room with my basketball.

And back in my office I made a decision. I am never showing Rebecca how I can spin a basketball on my finger. Ever. Even if she begs me to.

Unless she begs a whole lot. Then maybe.

But tonight, it's her loss.

Biblical Origins of Democrats and Republicans

A few years ago, I had the honor of sitting next to former Ohio Representative Tony Hall, who spoke at Kentucky's prayer breakfast.

He's a faithful and inspirational leader, and we discussed a range of serious topics before I inevitably had to try to inject some humor into our conversation.

Rep. Hall had a wonderful sense of humor, and inevitably the discussion turned to the bitter partisanship that was dividing our country.

There was a mix of Republicans and Democrats at the dinner. We wondered aloud where this division started.

I offered my theory that the Biblical story of the Prodigal Son may help answer that question.

The Prodigal Son was wasteful, extravagant, and disrespectful but returned home humbled and wiser, and was embraced and forgiven by his father who welcomed the lost son back and called for a celebration at his son's return.

The Prodigal Son also had an elder brother who had stayed home, worked hard, and was respectful and not wasteful but who watched on with jealousy and bitterness as the father embraced and extravagantly rewarded the formerly wayward younger son.

My theory is that Democrats descended from the Prodigal Son and Republicans descended from his brother.

Although Biblically and politically I was on shaky ground, we at least laughed together and agreed the reasons for our differences were probably about as trivial and the ability to bridge them about as simple.

Don't Fret the Imaginary

A few years back during the winter months we had a snow storm that caused my work to close down for the day. My son, Johnny, was about 9 or 10 years old and excited Dad was getting to stay home from work and wanted me to join him outside to play in the snow.

He first asked me around 10am that morning and I responded, "Johnny, I will...but right now the stock market is down over 200 points. I want to see what is happening and monitor a little longer. Give me another hour and check back with me."

An hour passed and back Johnny came ready for the snow. "Johnny," I said, "the stock market is now down 300 points and I don't know what is going on. Can you please give me a little more time and check back around noon?"

Noon came around and in came Johnny. Again. "Dad, how is the stock market going?" I responded, "Johnny, this is awful. The market is now down over 500 points. Unbelievable."

Johnny paused for a moment and then said, "Why does it matter so much? Mom just told me we don't own any stocks."

"Yeah," I said. "Well, you know... that may be true. We really don't own any stocks right now. So it really doesn't matter much to us.

We then went outside and played in the snow. And I didn't worry about the stock market plummeting the rest of the day.

Nietzsche v. Brown

"If you stare long enough into the abyss, the abyss will stare back at you."—Friedrich Nietzsche

"But if you stare a little longer into the abyss, it will wink at you and you will both giggle simultaneously."—John Y Brown III

Running Away from Home to Find It

I always wanted to live in a big city –or so I thought. I finally got my wish at age 19 when I moved to Los Angeles, California, to attend the University of Southern California. I was excited about attending a big name school like USC, but I was even more excited about living in one of the largest and most alluring cities in the world, Los Angeles, California.

I didn't know much about LA and was just excited to be a kid from Kentucky moving into the big city and trying to fit in.

I remember one of the first night's there watching the David Letterman Show with this eccentric author named Quentin Crisp, with a purple streak in his graying hair, as a guest who summed up the differences between Los Angeles and New York City, "Los Angeles is an endless sunny paradise where everyone is beautiful and rich and awards grow on trees. But if you want to rule the world, you have to live in New York."

Clearly, Los Angeles was a "beautiful people" town, and although I wasn't really cut out for that, I wanted badly to fit in.

My first week moving in, a female student from UCLA made conversation with me at a party and then asked her female friend to come over to talk to me. I was nervous and excited but ultimately disappointed when I realized why she summoned her friend.

"Oh my God, listen to him talk. Say something. He's got the most country accent. Say something."

They then asked where I was from and I told them Kentucky.

"Is that a state?" she asked.

I said, "No, Kentucky was a small city in Nashville, which was a state next to Tennessee."

No one laughed, so I finally explained the joke. And no one laughed again. Although I was asked to repeat parts of it so they could hear my country accent.

I went to the beach a lot the first few weeks. I didn't surf or know how to hang out at the beach like other guys in LA my age. I tried to up my game by using something called "Sun-In" to lighten my hair, to make it blonder and more LA-ish.

It worked well the first day. And second day. The third day I rubbed it in like shampoo. And it turned my hair into a very intense shade of blonde. But most people would just call it orange. Fortunately for me, orange hair wasn't as out of place in LA as it would have been back home in Louisville or Lexington I just went with it and was told by a friend it would eventually grow out and that "it wasn't obviously orange," which helped but only a little.

So, I looked like a meek Southern boy who had just moved to LA and tried to fit in by bleaching his hair blonde but failed and accidentally dyed it orange.

I was not off to an auspicious start blending in to the LA beautiful people scene. After a month or so, I was learning my way around and my orange hair was starting to grow out (making a kind of cool-looking orange-with-brown-roots combination).

I was settling in and figured it was time to find a local doctor just in case I ever needed medical help. My mother suggested I get our local doctor to recommend a general practitioner, but stubborn, independent, and orange-headed, I decided I would find my own West Coast doctor. I did so by using the yellow pages and finding a doctor nearest my apartment.

Having passed my test for proximity, I confidently called my new GP and made an appointment to meet him and get a physical.

As part of the physical, he took a blood sample and then I was given a cup to, well, you know. The doctor explained I was to take the cup to the lab. I wasn't sure what room number he gave but didn't want to be rude and ask him to repeat it. It sounded like the room was two floors up. I walked outside, holding my sample, and took the elevator up. I went into the office I thought I was told to go to and knocked on the receptionist's screen. It was about 5 pm and they were closing. The attractive receptionist opened up the screen and said, "Hallloo" in a lovely French accent.

I swallowed hard and held up my specimen and said, "Hello" in my unconfident Southern accent adding, "I think I'm supposed to leave this with you."

She smiled and laughed. "No" and pointed to the sign just below her that indicated I was at a dentist's office.

"Oh, OK. I'm so sorry! I'm really, really sorry" again with my Southern accent.

I wanted to add that the orange in my hair was growing out and would look normal again soon, but didn't.

She did give me the room number for the lab, which was actually next door to the doctor's office I just left.

So I went back to the elevator holding my sample in complete defeat as the elevator doors opened. About seven or eight very LA-like attractive secretaries were on the elevator leaving for the day. And there I was, in my Kentucky version of an LA outfit holding a urine specimen in my right hand. The two in front giggled but tried to look away. I should have told them to go ahead and I would wait for the next elevator but I was too embarrassed to think and just stepped on and tried to find a pocket on my jacket to hide my sample but couldn't and just stood there mortified.

As I stepped off the elevator, I heard more giggling. And as the door closed, I looked down the long hall which seemed longer and narrower than it really was and walked with my head spinning and stomach turning.

I was reminded of the Quintin Crisp quote about LA being a different kind of place created by and for the beautiful and rich. I figured if I wanted to fit in and be happy somewhere, I would eventually have to move back to my home state of Kentucky. Which really isn't a small city in the state of Nashville next to Tennessee. But is an awfully fine place to live.

I didn't move back home immediately, but sensed after that day that it was just a matter of time before I would. I finished several semesters at USC and even made the Dean's List and declared a major in philosophy but never lost my accent.

My orange hair did grow out and I managed to adjust enough to function adequately and not stand out but never quite fit in. I got to explore LA – or LaLa Land as some call it-- and had some exciting experiences, quite a few, in fact.

Los Angeles is a good place to go to collect unique, dramatic and intense experiences but not a great place to connect. That was the one thing I seemed to have in common with others. I remember reading somewhere that LA is a place where a lot of people live lonely together.

My favorite quote about LA, though, was "LA is a great city to date but Minneapolis is a better city to marry." Or Louisville, in my case.

As much as I thought I wanted to live in a big city, I realized I valued not being lonely even more. And after my tour in LA, headed home.

I did learn you fit in best where you most belong and I was glad to get back to Kentucky. We Kentuckians have a strong sense of home and even a famous state song celebrating it.

In one of my first college classes back in Louisville, the professor asked each of us to introduce ourselves. I did so and explained I had transferred from USC.

"Oh, so I guess you decided you wanted to be a big fish in a small pond rather than a small fish in a big pond?" the professor asked.

"Nah," I shrugged. "I decided I wanted to be a medium-sized fish in a medium-sized pond."

The 27th Anniversary of the Day that My Life Changed

The day –or night, really-- that my life changed. Not because of something I did. But because of something harmful I stopped doing.

We never know what the markers in our life will look like. The last time we pass a certain street, see a certain friend, or embrace a loved one. We only find out afterwards and try to make sense of it after the fact.

Which is what happened to me on this night exactly 27 years ago. In fact, it was October 18th at around 2:30 am.

I had moved back home with my mother and was a listless, beleaguered, and bewildered soul. I thought a string of bad luck I had recently endured had led me to drink excessively.

Turns out, I had the string of bad luck because I was drinking excessively.

I was up late alone watching the movie Reuben, Reuben again. It was a movie about a rumpled, drunken curly haired poet who had traded whatever talent he once had to sponge off others he was happy to take advantage of—and time was running out for him. I suspect at the time I believed I related to something noble in his character, some potential he had but was throwing away. In retrospect, I related to the excessive drinking, manipulation of others, and mostly frittering away of a life that could much more. In the final scene (after the one below), Reuben attempts suicide and, before he can change his mind, accidentally dies.

That night 27 years ago after the movie ended, I walked the last bottles of booze out to the condo's garbage chute and ceremoniously dropped them down one by one. And walked back inside.

And I have not had a drink of alcohol since.

It was perhaps my life's most important turning point. I have never seen the movie since, but every October 18th I think of it. And thank God that the end of that movie also ended a misguided and unfortunate period in my life. And that I have since—as a result of leaving booze out of my life—led a life that has given me the "much more" I sensed I was losing.

Why do I mention this?

I don't say it to boast. Removing behavior that harms yourself and your loved ones, is not praise-worthy as much as common sense—and the least you'd expect of yourself. I suppose I share this because I know there are others out there tonight who feel alienated, lost, and confused and who may even be romanticizing destructive behavior by drinking to escape it all.

To them I hope to say, There is nothing heroic or romantic about wasting your life and hurting others.

And if you don't agree, I believe you are confusing desperation for depth and self-absorption for self-reliance. And foolhardiness for uniqueness. And you are probably going to be the last person in the room to realize this. And that's OK. You are, like me, about average. And that's a good thing. Because help is available. More help than ever in history.

And all you have to do to access it is to set aside the brilliant future you falsely imagine for yourself long enough to notice the unbearable reality of your present circumstances—and then pick up the phone and dial directory assistance on the telephone.

And then don't hang up until you ask for the help you need.

And then breathe a sigh of relief that the awful movie of your current life is about to end. And a new story about your real future is about to begin.

And the new story of your life will still star you—not as an actor playing some imaginary part you thought you were supposed to. Rather, it will be you simply playing yourself, which is a much more natural role that will introduce you to yourself. And it will allow those same people in the room to finally get to be around the person they've been waiting for. And here's the best part: Eventually, you'll come to like this person too.

The new movie could be about how to appreciate the poetry of a life lived by humbly following our better instincts rather than merely rhyming words in the intoxicated hope of sounding clever. Or just about anything we want it to be.

I hope you don't miss out on it. I'm grateful every day—but especially on this day every year—that I am not missing out on mine.

What Thanksgiving are you Most Thankful For?

I asked myself this question today and the answer was immediate and obvious but not what you might expect. It was Thanksgiving 34 years ago. I was 21 and we were having Thanksgiving, as we always did, at my maternal grandmother and grandfather's home in Central City in Muhlenberg County.

I always looked forward to seeing my cousins, aunts and uncles and visiting my Uncle Tommy, who was quadriplegic and probably my favorite relative, and I always loved being with my grandparents, who I spent much of my childhood with.

My grandparents' home in Central City was my refuge. My sanctuary. And during Thanksgiving it was a fun refuge and sanctuary. But on Thanksgiving in 1984 I was deeply lost in an addiction to alcohol.

I was supposed to arrive early that afternoon but chose drinking with friends and later alone instead of leaving on time. I stopped several times on the way down to have a few more drinks.

There were no cell phones at the time, so I called from pay phones at truck stops with phony excuses about why I was running behind..

I arrived long after dark and too late to visit with my Uncle Tommy, a tradition we had on Thanksgiving eve.

I still remember what I was wearing, a blue pull-over sweat suit top and jeans. I looked grungy and felt grungy because I was grungy.

I tried to clean up just before arriving, gulping down coffee and putting Visine in my eyes. It was a routine I was used to that never worked as well as I imagined.

When I finally arrived, everyone seemed happy to see me but also had a subtle concern in their eyes. I tried to make up in charm and humor what I had lost in integrity and self-respect. I sat on the dinner table and

138

explained to family members interested in listening my made up story about why I was nearly six hours late.

But it was just another story and just one more time I was bringing sadness and concern to a family gathering rather than something pleasant or hopeful.

I had a large bottle of scotch hidden in my overnight bag and throughout the evening would slip back to my bedroom to sneak a few drinks.

The next morning when everyone was saying goodbye, I was nowhere to be found. I was sitting in the driveway alone in my car listening to music blocking out everyone and everything. Alcoholism is a lonely disease.

My grandmother told me several years later when I apologized to her that she was worried about "Her John" and had known something was wrong with me but wasn't sure what it was.

The reason this Thanksgiving is my most memorable is it was the Thanksgiving I was most disgusted with the person I had allowed myself to become. Disgusted enough to never want to repeat it.

A short time afterward, I agreed to get help for my drinking and for the past 33 Thanksgivings, I have been present and sober and, most importantly, able to be myself and hopefully added rather than subtracted from family festivities.

I mention this on our national holiday for giving thanks because many of us today may not be feeling very thankful at all. Some may feel lost and alienated or full of self-loathing and despair --- and that may not be a bad thing. The bottom can sometimes also be the beginning. If you are struggling with addiction, it can be a time when you finally decide to make a change in your life, possibly a dramatic change. And if you do, this seemingly sad holiday moment may become the Thanksgiving you are one day, like me, the most thankful for.

RIP Phillip Seymour Hoffman

Phillip Seymour Hoffman mesmerized me every time his character walked onto the screen.

He was, in my opinion, one of the greatest actors in my lifetime, and I am sad he is gone from us.

He died of a drug overdose with a needle stuck in his arm at the young age of 46.

Phillip Seymour Hoffman in addition to being one of our greatest artists was also a garden variety drug addict who got help in his early 20s and stayed clean for 23 years before falling off the wagon last year.

He thought he could pull off the performance of a lifetime by using drugs again even though he was an addict.

All addicts are actors, of course. They have to be to juggle their double-life until they get help or time runs out.

And that applies to even one of the very greatest actors among us. And today time ran out on him.

I am sad Phillip Seymour Hoffman died. He meant something to me. My heart went out to him every time he appeared on screen. His presence would remind me of something missing in me and I would be reassured that I would be alright since he seemed alright.

But that scary something missing in him –and missing in so many of us– can sometimes get the best of us. If we don't know what to fill it with.

A True Hero for Our World

Our world seems on the cusp of losing a genuine hero for the ages, Nelson Mandela.

The word hero gets overused a lot but never when applied Mr. Mandela, who looks like Morgan Freeman playing God after God decided to stick around and live among the mortals.

Muhammad Ali famously dismissed achieving the impossible saying "Impossible is nothing." Nelson Mandela has exemplified that statement throughout his life and continues to do so.

I first heard of Nelson Mandela when I was 20 years old and got to spend several days in South Africa in 1983. Apartheid, legalized racial discrimination against blacks, was embedded in the nation's legal system. Nelson Mandela was incarcerated and in poor health. We were told at the time that he would almost certainly die in prison.

But he didn't.

Several years later celebrating his 70th birthday while still in prison, Nelson Mandela rallied his people. He became a symbol of patient and peaceful persistence against injustice and a symbol of inspiration much like Mahatma Gandhi and Martin Luther King had become resisting injustices in their own countries just decades earlier.

Shortly after that, even though struggling with tuberculosis, Nelson Mandela emerged from prison a free man who not only physically survived but lived to become the president of his country and the first black office holder in South African history.

Ironically, his country had imprisoned him years earlier for resisting its laws and committing treason and sedition in defying Apartheid during his youth. As president of South Africa, Nelson Mandela removed the yoke of Apartheid from his country.

And today, nearly 30 years after I first heard Mandela's name whispered as a ghost in the failed resistance to South Africa's Apartheid policy, he has become the living embodiment of everything that was impossible then

How does that happen?

How does a man physically broken, legally incarcerated, politically written off, ill with a potentially fatal malady and aging into his 70s not give up?

How does that same man emerge in his twilight years to become arguably an even more successful South African version of our nation's Abraham Lincoln?

I don't know.

Except that's the kind of thing that real heroes do --and real heroes are as rare as they are extraordinary. And this extraordinary hero is still alive and in our midst. Although sadly, not for much longer. But he's here now.

And we are blessed to be able to acknowledge him, again, while he is still alive. And thank him for teaching us that impossible isn't always as difficult to overcome as it may seem.

Memories of a True Kentucky Statesman

I want to share a few memories about Gatewood Galbraith, a Kentucky statesman, who died recently in his sleep.

I don't claim to have known Gatewood as a good friend, but he was much more to me than a casual acquaintance. I ran in several statewide races alongside Gatewood.

Political candidates are a bit like athletes traveling together across the state, appearing to shake hands and give speeches wherever two or more registered voters are gathered. There is a camaraderie that develops. And a respect and friendship that lasts. As a young man I knew Gatewood the way everyone else knew him, as the hilarious, unrestrained, whip-smart, loquacious character who added comic relief and trenchant insights to Kentucky's governor's races.

In one of the first debates I watched with Gatewood, he defended medicinal marijuana by saying something along the lines of "We aren't talking about people who get drunk, cross state lines, and trash hotel rooms. We are talking about people who will mellow out and order a pizza and fall asleep."

But because he wanted to legalize medicinal marijuana (coupled with the fact he looked like he just dressed himself and shaved from the backseat of his car), he was never taken as seriously as he could have been. And I wondered how seriously he wanted to be taken. Gatewood could have been an able governor had he ever found a way to get elected, but I'm not sure he really ran to win. I think he ran because he couldn't not run and because he had something to say and people wanted to hear it. And it beat practicing law seven days a week.

And he was good at running for office—extraordinary, in fact. It just made sense for Gatewood to run. And keep running. And because of that, he mattered a lot to a lot of people across our great state.

The first time I seriously reflected on Gatewood's politics, I was in college. A friend of mine at University of Louisville was taking a political science class on Kentucky politics, and Gatewood was used as an example along with my grandfather, John Y Brown, Sr., as two Kentucky politicians who ran often for office and rarely won, but who managed to shape the debate and affect policy in important ways.

Well, I wasn't too crazy about that characterization, but I agreed there was something to it. They were alike in some important ways as political influencers, except Gatewood had the good sense never to win a race.

My grandfather never smoked pot that I know of and probably never advocated for legalizing it, but he would have respected and liked Gatewood and considered him a man with who had ideas worth listening to and thinking about.

My first personal encounter with Gatewood was in the 1995 Democratic primary. I was running for secretary of state, and Gatewood was running for governor. We were in a small town in Northern Kentucky at a speaking engagement. It was a disappointing turnout. There were more candidates attending than voters. I joked in my speech that I might not have persuaded anyone in the audience to vote for me, but I thought I picked up Gatewood and two auditor candidates that night as supporters.

I was a newcomer to politics and needed some wise counsel that evening. Unlike most any other candidate seriously running for office, I chose Gatewood to consult with. "Gatewood, I need your advice on something important. Do you have a minute?"

"Sure, Johnny! What can I do for you?"

"Well, Gatewood, I'm struggling to raise money in my race. I hate it, but I know it's important. I received a check yesterday from Joe Smith (a fictional name) for $500 and I was overjoyed—but there's a problem. Joe went to prison a few years ago on a drug-related charge. He's out now and doing well, but I'm worried about accepting a campaign contribution from him. What should I do?"

Gatewood put his arm around me and we walked away from the crowd. In his own friendly yet also fatherly way, he intoned, "Johnny, Joe Smith is a dear friend of mine. I was with Joe at his going-away party the night before he went to prison. But Johnny, not even I could take a check from Joe Smith. You have to give it back." I did, and I was always grateful for that advice.

During my eight years as secretary of state, I was by virtue of that office, the state's chief election officer who registered all candidates who ran for statewide office. As a result, I got to see Gatewood a lot during that time.

There was Gatewood's affiliation with Woody Harrelson, who was speaking out about legalizing hemp and had just starred as Kentucky's own Larry Flynt in The People vs Larry Flynt. Woody came down to our office several times before or after a press conference in the capitol rotunda. Politicians typically love the chance to get to hang out with a celebrity—especially if the cameras are rolling and it appears the celebrity is somehow approving of you. But usually not if the celebrity is trying to legalize illegal substances and just starred in a movie as the king of porn, albeit a native son. I enjoyed getting to meet Woody Harrelson, but I was painfully cautious in avoiding ever being caught on camera with him. Gatewood welcomed and relished the affiliation. On principle and genuine friendship.

Another particular visit stands out in my mind. Gatewood came by to ask about filing requirements for some office, I think attorney general. He took his hat off and sat down across from my desk and smiled in that broad and easy Gatewood way.

"How you doing, Gatewood?" I asked.

"I'm doing great, Johnny. It's a good age for me right now… I just turned 55. The world gets bigger and life gets better. I just left a lovely lady who is about my age and she was with her mother and daughter. I gotta tell you, Johnny, I was equally attracted to all three of them. Life is good. Anyway, I think it may be time for me to run for attorney general. What do you think?"

Who was I ever to argue with a loaded question like that?

In 2007 I ran for lieutenant governor and Gatewood for governor. He had hit his stride and just written his now famous book, The Last Free Man in America. We had fun and funny memories traveling the state again. I traveled four to five hours at a time to give speeches in the most remote parts of Kentucky. Gatewood was always there. Always. And always dazzled the crowd with his oratory and good will. And he was often the first to arrive, the last to leave, or both. He had a genuine passion for what he was doing and an infectious love of life.

My last interaction with Gatewood was about 5 months ago during the 2011 governor's race. I had just gotten my hair cut at a men's hair salon I was trying for the first time. I was paying and making conversation with the talkative shop manager. She was full of life, too, and carrying on about Frankfort politics. She said, "You know that guy who ran for governor and wrote a book? I love him. What's his name?" I thought for a minute and said, "Jonathan Miller?"

"No, I don't think so. He's wild. I just love him and would give anything to meet him someday." "Gatewood Galbraith? I asked." "Yes, oh my God, that's him! Do you know him?"

I told her I did and would call and see if he could come by and say hello.

Half an hour later I had called Dea Riley, Gatewood's lieutenant governor running mate and she called Gatewood who said he would be at the hair salon to meet this young fan next Wednesday—but that he couldn't get his haircut there because he had used the same barber in Lexington for decades. Gatewood called me the next day to confirm and asked if I could join him and I said yes. Something came up, though, and he couldn't make it in but still called the shop and spoke to the manager who was so excited to get to talk to Gatewood and Dea.

And that's the way I remember Gatewood. He made a young person's day by caring enough to say hello and talk politics and policy. And make a new friend. Because he wanted to and it was the right way to treat people.

Gatewood Galbraith was, indeed, the last free man in America— in more ways than he even knew.

A Fancy Farm Memory

Kentucky has a constitutional oath that requires officeholders to swear they won't fight in a duel. Yet at the same time Kentucky has the political crucible of Fancy Farm that requires candidates seeking statewide and congressional office are required to endure each August — which at times has seemed less inviting than a duel with guns.

It's not bullets you fear but jeers and cheers (for your opponent) and the momentary mental lapse or twist of tongue that could be the gaffe that everyone talks about the next day. You fear humiliation on the most prized of our state's political stages, the platform for political speeches at Fancy Farm.

Fancy farm is an amalgam of history and entertainment. Part historic and revered much like the old Chautauqua assembly and yet also part "trial by ordeal" much like the carnival game of baseball toss to cause the seated person to fall into the dunking tank. As a speaker at Fancy Farm you strive to be remembered as falling into the former category rather than into the metaphorical dunking tank. And if you succeed, you are the exception to the rule.

At 32, I was the Democratic Party's nominee for secretary of state and slated to speak at the vaunted Fancy Farm picnic. The picnic is on a Saturday and I was staying in Paducah, Kentucky the entire week before leading up to Fancy Farm to campaign in the Western Kentucky region and prepare mentally for the big day. As the big day approached, the more nervous I got. Thursday I was barely able to eat. To make matters worse, it was my anniversary and, yes, I somehow blanked out and forgot. My wife had not forgotten. Fortunately, with the help of some wonderful local friends we found a romantic restaurant in Paducah to spend our 4th anniversary together. And after that romantic dinner, and the gift of a kitchen table my wife had been lobbying me to buy us for several months, I salvaged our big day as best I could under the circumstances.

The next day was the Democratic Party's Bean Supper in Marshall County, a major event as part of the run up to Fancy Farm. It was my first visit to Marshall County since the primary and I got off to a rocky start after I announced to the large audience that it was "Great to be back in McCracken County again." After the speech the chair of the Democratic Party whispered to me that I was actually in Marshall County. I asked if I should get back on stage and correct myself and maybe explain it was confusing with both counties starting with the letter "M" but he suggested I just let it lie and work on getting it right next year.

I also learned after my less than dazzling speech that swung for the fences and at best turned out to be a broken bat single that sometimes less is more on the speaking stump. I spoke after attorney general candidate and current state auditor Ben Chandler. My speech was all over the place as I tried too hard to stand out. Afterward I asked Ben how I did. He leaned over and whispered to me, "You know, it's not always the best strategy to try to give the most memorable speech at Fancy Farm."

I wasn't quite sure what Ben meant at that moment but soon learned. The next day I saw Ben's opponent, Will T Scott, become overly passionate as he got caught up in the moment of the intensely dramatic Fancy Farm experience –in the same way US Senate Candidate Scotty Baesler did a few years later — and footage from both speeches found their way into damaging commercial spots that made them looked unhinged.

That evening after the Bean Supper we went by Fancy Farm to get a sense of the layout and what we should expect the next day. As we pulled in I got a call from my father that he and my step-mother of 17 years were getting divorced. I gave my condolences to both and after talking through it best we could, I hung up the phone after we agreed to talk more about it on Monday. I got out of the car and approached the podium. I was greeted by Al Cross, Kentucky's gold standard for political reporting and someone who somehow manages to find out things happening in your life even before they happen—or often before you find out about it. "Hi John," Al offered. "Hello, Al. Good to see you," even though as a political candidate seeing Al approach you really doesn't feel good.

Getting interviewed by Al Cross was a civilized and erudite prelude to Fancy Farm in many ways. Another political right of passage in Kentucky but without noisemakers to excuse a poor response. And there was good reason to fear Al. He almost always knew more about the topic than you did—despite the fact you were supposed to have mastered the issue as a candidate. Al would find a way to always ask the tough question you'd hoped he had forgotten and ask it in a diplomatic way. He was always fair. But that was the problem with Al. Politicians aren't all that keen on just getting fair treatment in the media. We prefer reporting that depicts us as a mirror image of how we view ourselves which is aspirational not objective. But it news coverage doesn't work that way, especially with Al Cross, the consummate political umpire in our state.

"Do you have any comment on your father and step-mother's divorce?" Al asked.

I thought to myself, "My goodness. I just found out less than 2 minutes ago myself!" I mumbled something like, "I love them both and they are both good people who are moving in separate directions and I wish them well and will always consider Phyllis family."

I had already learned from Ben Chandler the night before to say less and stop. Like everything in life, with politics and the Fancy Farm experience, you learn as you go.

The next day I paced a lot. If anyone had taken my pulse or blood pressure they would have been concerned for my health. But Fancy Farm is like preparing for a giant Bungee jump. The adrenaline is needed and welcomed. When I was introduced I had already taken off my jacket, rolled up my sleeves, and just hoped I didn't forget how to walk from my chair to the podium. I didn't use my notes and had memorized my speech but tried to make it seem extemporaneous. It went very well. As I finished I remember looking down at the crowd and seeing a seasoned pol and mentor cheering me on. My wife was standing and cheering (even after the forgotten anniversary debacle). Even though I had risen to speak as a meek candidate for a mid-level office, I sat down feeling like a battle-tested pro. It was the rush of a lifetime. And I had succeeded. For the moment.

My opponent, Steve Crabtree, spoke next and I tried looking at the audience and just hoping he'd just finish his speech and sit down so I could bask more confidently in my momentary Fancy Farm survival glory. But something unexpected happened. Steve began making references about my father and holding up the book The Bluegrass Conspiracy, a sensational book that contained damaging allegations about my father. Most were false but this wasn't a court of law. It was the carnival-like no-holds-barred Fancy Farm theater.

My opponent was holding a copy of the controversial book as republicans in the audience applauded and howled approvingly and then he proceeded to walk over the Democratic side of the podium.

This was my moment of truth. Would I handle this political provocation in a mature and controlled manner? Of course I wouldn't.

At first I pretended to yawn and joke with the crowd as I waved my hand dismissively at Steve Crabtree's fulminating speech. But the chanting got under my skin and my youthful temper flared and without being fully aware of what I was doing, all 5 '9 of me stood up suddenly as though I was expecting stare down my 6 '3 opponent. Fortunately for me, the democratic candidate for agriculture commissioner and then the democratic candidate for governor, restrained me from embarrassing myself and I walked to the back of the podium to cool off before doing something foolish.

My momentary glory had spiraled into a side show of my own making. I had made my mark at Fancy Farm but it wasn't in the way I had hoped. Oddly, though, it wasn't a total bust as I demonstrated to the rowdy crowd that I did have a lot of fight in me and wouldn't stand for another person to criticize my family.

I found my opponent afterwards and asked if he would speak to me for a few minutes and he agreed. I laughed and said "I can't believe I stood up like I was going to punch you. You are twice my size, for goodness sakes!"

He chuckled and said slyly, "If you had, it would have been the lead story tomorrow instead of a curious footnote. I was hoping you would." Again, I learned that keeping your cool is paramount at Fancy Farm.

I also learned the even more valuable lesson of when you say something untrue about another person, you admit it, correct it and apologize for it immediately. I apologized to Steve Crabtree for making a misstatement about his personal life the night before and he graciously accepted my apology.

As we left the Fancy Farm grounds, I saw a political insider and friend who approached me laughing heartily. He hugged me and said, "Well, you just lost your political virginity today, didn't you?"

I suppose I had. I left Fancy Farm feeling like a survivor intact and that was good enough for me.

Perhaps my proudest accomplishment from my first Fancy Farm is that after the campaign ended I stayed in touch with my former political opponent Steve Crabtree. I again apologized for my mistake and he apologized for roughhousing me rhetorically from the Fancy Farm podium. We have kept in touch over the ensuing 24 years. He is a good man and an even better father and husband and has a distinguished career in broadcast journalism. I am proud to call him a friend and worthy foe and know he feels the same about me.

So, after all the fanfare and hoopla; after all the air horns and caterwauling, and after the brave speeches that may or may not be heard or understood, there is something lasting we don't always easily see that transpires from Fancy Farm. The bonding of the characters who shined or were shunned or who simply survived day's spectacle. They become bigger yet humbler people by surviving the political ordeal of Fancy Farm and that is an important legacy worth preserving.

Supremely Disappointing

I grew up believing that the Supreme Court was our most vaunted institution -- the final and independent arbiter of the US Constitution, to which we claim fealty as the foundation for governing our glorious and complex nation -- and that the job of the US Senate was to protect steadfastly the sanctity of the Court no matter how strong or tempting the political winds.

The politicization of the Supreme Court was inevitable but was never to be joined by -- or God forbid, led by -- the body that took a sworn oath to protect its integrity and independence. In recent years, the Senate has dropped even the pretense that our highest court is anything but a partisan prize to be secured by one political side at the expense of the other.

Supreme Court nominees have always had a degree of partisan bias. They are selected by partisan presidents. But competence and scholarship superseded the political, especially in the confirmation process. Until several decades ago.

Both sides are fully complicit and culpable in the debasing of the Senate's constitutional role of providing impartial advice and consent for Supreme Court nominees. And seeking to affix greater blame to Democrats or Republicans misses the point and only ensures that the political escalation of the Supreme Court continues.

This past week's histrionics are, in my view, merely a curious footnote to the larger and sadder spectacle of the abnegation by the US Senate of their trusted role as chief protector of our most critical institution.

What we as a nation have been debating the past week-- what Brett Kavanaugh did or didn't mean when writing about drinking excesses in his high school yearbook -- avoided the more important question of whether the US Senate will ever again behave like sober adults rather than politically intoxicated adolescents when providing advice and consent to Supreme Court nominees.

From demagoguing Robert Bork to dispensing with Senate protocol and tradition to derail a nominee, the past 30 years of Senate confirmation hearings read more like puerile antics worthy of being scrawled boastfully in the back of a high school yearbook rather than statecraft worthy of the Congressional Record.

So does this mean Brett Kavanaugh is a good or bad choice for a lifetime appointment to the US Supreme Court?

It means the real question is whether Brett Kavanaugh will be the last member of the Court in its final gasp of judicial independence or the first member of the new iteration of the Supreme Court as a politically engineered entity.

US Senators on both sides of the aisle are behaving as though it's certainly the latter. And they should know. They have worked steadfastly the past 30 years to redesign the Court to be precisely that.

I Raise My Hand

I've listened to a lot of lectures the past couple of days on civility from both sides of the political aisle and am unmoved by the passionate finger pointing, no matter how well intentioned.

The criticism of others may make us feel better in the short run but it doesn't seem to improve things in the longer run.

I keep thinking back on a college class from several decades ago. The course was titled American Government and the topic was civil rights and race. The white professor began the lecture by asking:

"Who here holds some racist beliefs? Even if it is just a small attitude of bias about other races? C'mon. We all do. I do. Let's see a show of hands."

He raised his hand and slowly, one by one, every student in the class -- of every color and nationality -- raised his or her hand.

I didn't want to raise my hand. My grandfather had sponsored and championed Kentucky's Civil Rights Act, for goodness sake. But I had to admit my self-serving resistance didn't ring entirely true to me and I raised my hand.

There we all were, hands raised, admitting we each had our own personal biases against one another based on race, just before we began discussing the racial injustices that led to the Civil Rights Act.

It was a refreshing and humbling exercise that led to a more honest and respectful discussion on a very sensitive and difficult topic.

Today, listening to all the overheated rhetoric from both sides about political biases (seeing political opponents as personal enemies who are dispensable or deplorable --in short, who are less valuable as people), kept taking me back to that class.

instead of more self-righteous finger pointing --which only escalates incivility --- what if we imagined being asked:

"Who out there has political biases which cause them to believe that those who disagree with them are less worthy as people? Even if it is just a small attitude of political bias. C'mon. We all do. I do. Let's see a show of hands."

And what if once hands were raised, figuratively speaking, we each challenged ourselves not to blame anyone or anything else until we were able honestly to put our own hand down?

It would get quiet for a while and we'd probably be far more humble and respectful when we tried to discuss this sensitive and difficult topic.

I don't want to raise my hand and have good reasons why I don't think I am part of the problem. But I have to admit my self-serving resistance doesn't ring entirely true to me and I raise my hand.

John Y. Brown, III

John Y. Brown, III was born into a family dedicated to serving Kentucky in many ways, including the arena of public service. John's grandfather served in the U.S. Congress under FDR and as Kentucky's Speaker of the House. His father served as governor of Kentucky from 1979-1983. So it almost seemed inevitable that John would serve the commonwealth: in 1995 he was elected Kentucky's Secretary of State at the age of 32. Re-elected without opposition, he served a second term ending in 2003.

His accomplishments as secretary of state include:

- "Best Practice" by the National Governor's Association for a program that helped new businesses.
- Two terms as Chair of National Association of Secretaries of State Elections Committee.
- Led National Election Reform Task Force that prompted the Help America Vote Act
- Won numerous e-government awards for innovation in delivering government services.

Before entering politics, John headed up franchising for Roaster's Inc., developing fast food venues in 37 states and several foreign countries.

More recently, John served as vice president of ResCare, working in government relations for the Louisville-based human services company with over 40,000 employees in over 40 states and several foreign countries. He loves sharing his enthusiasm for business and law and served as an adjunct professor at Bellarmine University in Louisville. In 2007, John ran unsuccessfully as the lieutenant governor running mate on a ticket with gubernatorial candidate Jody Richards, Kentucky's Speaker of the House, in a spirited, seven-slate Democratic primary.

This combination of business, government, legal, and academic experience prepared John perfectly for the birth of the JYB3 Group, a firm dedicated to bringing the best of commerce and government together for the benefit of all Kentuckians. The JYB3 Group quickly became Kentucky's fastest growing public affairs firm.

The JYB3 Group recently celebrated their 10th anniversary and has been recognized as the "Best Very Small Business" in the Greater Louisville region (with 1-9 employees) and is the Kentucky member for TAG (The Advocacy Group), the premier municipal, state, federal and international government and public affairs organization in the world.

John also serves as Of Counsel for the law firm Kaplan, Johnson, Abate & Bird where he heads the firm's government relations practice.

John graduated magna cum laude from Bellarmine University where he earned a B.A in History and Philosophy, as well as an M.B.A., and earned his J.D cum laude from the University of Kentucky College of Law.

John met his wife Rebecca Brown 31 years ago at a Kentucky Derby party and they have been together ever since and married 27 years. They have two wonderful children who are the joy of their lives, John Y. Brown IV, 24, who has a BA in Economics and an MBA from Bellarmine University and is currently in law school at the University of Kentucky, and Maggie Brown, a music major and musical performer who is a junior at Elon University in North Carolina.

Made in the USA
Columbia, SC
02 April 2019